THE LADIES OF LYDIARD

Lydiard House - home to the St. John family for more than 500 years.

The Ladies
of
Lydiard

FRANCES BEVAN

THE HOBNOB PRESS

First published in the United Kingdom in 2021

by The Hobnob Press,
8 Lock Warehouse,
Severn Road, Gloucester GL1 2GA
www.hobnobpress.co.uk

British Library Cataloguing in Publication Data
A catalogue record for this book is available from the British Library

ISBN 978-1-914407-02-4

Typeset in Adobe Garamond Pro 11/14 pt.
Typesetting and origination by John Chandler

Front cover: Anne Leighton, the first wife of Sir John St. John, 1st Bt.
Back cover: Lydiard House, the front lawn

Contents

Introduction to the Ladies of Lydiard

A COLLECTION OF magnificent portraits crowds the walls of the beautifully restored state rooms in Lydiard House, but when the Palladian mansion opened to the public for the first time in 1955 the rooms and the walls were all but bare. When Vernon Henry St. John 7th Viscount St. John and 6th Viscount Bolingbroke left his ancestral home for the last time, he took with him most of his family portraits. Then more than 20 years later he made a surprising gesture when he offered Swindon Corporation the opportunity to purchase 32 paintings, an offer they accepted with alacrity.

So, who were these St. John's and where did they hail from? The genealogical work of art on the polyptych in St Mary's Church, claims that John de St John entered England with the Conqueror. However, most St. John family historians believe it seems more probable that Roger St. John one of four brothers arrived in the 12th century during the reign of Henry I.

Oliver St. John was the first member of the family to acquire the Lydiard estate through his marriage to heiress Margaret Beauchamp. Oliver St. John who was born in about 1398 most probably at Paulerspury, Northamptonshire, traced his family line back to a 12th-century marriage between Lord William de Port and Godechild Paynel. William changed his name to St. John, that of his maternal grandmother, Muriel St. John, the daughter of Roger de St. John.

There were Ladies at Lydiard long before the arrival of the St. Johns but it was Oliver and his wife Margaret who put the family and the estate on the map. Margaret skilfully controlled both her fortune and her fate following Oliver's death in 1437 in Rouen,

Normandy. She carefully conveyed the estates she had brought to the marriage. Her eldest son John inherited from his mother the estates of Bletsoe and Keysoe in Bedfordshire along with Fonmon, Penmark, Barry and Llancadle in Glamorganshire from his father. Younger son Oliver received the manors of Garsington in Oxfordshire, Hatfield Peverel and Termynes in Essex with Deptford (Westgrenewich) in Kent and his mother's inheritance of Lydiard Manor.

The Lydiard estate once comprised more than 3,000 acres. In the mid-18th century, the St. John landholding in Wiltshire included the Manor of Lydiard Tregoze with land in the parish of Lydiard Tregoze and neighbouring Lydiard Millicent and Shaw, Poulton, Marlborough, Ogbourne St Andrew, Mildenhall, Bynol (Bincknoll), Broad Hinton, Cotmarsh, Chaddington and Clyffe Pypard. But by the mid-19th century it was a rather different story. While earlier generations of the family had been conscientiously safeguarding their inheritance, subsequent St. Johns were rather better at spending it.

And what about the Lydiard ladies who lived in this maelstrom of fluctuating finances? The St. John men were very adept at making influential marriages to wealthy women who brought property, money and profitable connections to the Welsh noblemen.

The Lydiard ladies lived under different conventions. They brought prestige and influence to their St. John marriages, but they enjoyed little independence, their inheritance immediately becoming the property of their husbands. They had no control over how their fortunes were spent or how they lived their lives. Or was that really what life was like for the Lydiard ladies?

Both Margaret Beauchamp and her daughter Margaret Beaufort controlled their fortunes and chose their own husbands in a period when it was unusual so to do while Anne, Countess Rochester hung on to her properties during the tumultuous period of the English Civil Wars, acting as a spymaster working with the Sealed Knot organisation and the exiled King Charles II.

But what about Lydiard House? Well, they either loved it or loathed it.

For Anne Leighton, the young wife of Sir John St. John 1st Baronet it was a family home when the St. John fortunes were flying high. She didn't survive to witness the catastrophic events of the Civil Wars that would ravage her family, claiming three of her sons.

Lady Johanna St. John spent most of her married life at Bolingbroke House in Battersea, but the Lydiard estate came in very handy for providing produce when the King came to dine and for entertaining her husband's influential friends.

For Anne Furnese it was her 'work in progress,' her husband's extravagant Grand Design while for poor, beleaguered Bessie Howard, the gamekeeper's granddaughter, it was a responsibility and a financial burden. For her keeping up appearances was probably the most difficult.

Today the 18th-century Viscounts, dressed in their parliamentary and coronation robes, look down their long St. John noses as visitors pass before them. Meeting their gaze from across the room are some of the ladies who supported them through good times and bad; ladies whose stories are seldom heard.

1

Lydiard House and St. Mary's Church

To set the scene for the lives of these Lydiard ladies, let us first visit the house in which they lived and the church where they worshipped.

For more than 800 years the Lydiard estate was owned by just five families. In the last decades of the 19th century the parish of Lydiard Tregoze consisted of a small village at Hook, Lydiard House and Park, St. Mary's Church, several small hamlets and numerous outlying farms and scattered cottages. The medieval village of Lydiard Tregoze was lost, most probably during an outbreak of plague in the first half of the 17th century. All that remained of the medieval landscape was the ancient hollow way, the former well-worn road between village and church, and the shadow of ridge and furrow ploughing in the fields.

Changes were made to the property in the 17th century, most probably by Sir John St. John, 1st Baronet, with extensions made to the original medieval manor house. Only one known image of Lydiard House predates the 18th-century remodelling. An illustration presently held by Warwick County Record Office shows a Tudor/Jacobean H-shaped house with single storey extensions built on the two wings and service rooms on the north west side. Three tree lined driveways criss-cross the estate, information which proved crucial to the landscape restoration work begun in 2004.

Henry, 1st Viscount St. John also made some structural changes to the house but it was his son John (Jack) St. John, 2nd Viscount St. John who made the most dramatic and enduring

A plunge pool or cold bath was built by George Richard 3rd Viscount Bolingbroke in about 1820 and rediscovered during excavation for the Lydiard Park project 2004-7.

changes to the Lydiard estate. The manor house was not so much rebuilt as remodelled and much of the original plan was abandoned due to cash flow problems.

With an intention of raising the family's standing in the county and with his wealthy wife's inheritance burning a hole in his pocket, Jack travelled around the west country studying other people's building projects such as that of the Earl of Pembroke at Wilton House, near Salisbury. He wanted to both modernise and impress, something he didn't achieve, according to his critical half-brother, Henry Viscount Bolingbroke.

By 1743 work was pretty much completed according to a commemorative plaque in the roof space. Jack remodelled the parkland and swept away the formal 17th-century features. Out went the bowling green and the gardens beloved by his grandmother Lady Johanna and in came the sweeping landscape vista made popular by Lancelot 'Capability' Brown. And that was pretty much it for the house for two hundred years, apart from some redecorating in 1828 when some expensive red flock wallpaper was hung in the Drawing Room and the State Bedroom. Minor repairs kept the place ticking over until even these ground to a halt.

When Lady Mary, the former Bessie Howard, died on 22 February 1940 the struggle to maintain the mortgaged estate came to an end. As the only surviving trustee of Lady Mary's will, her estate manager and cousin Edward Hiscock put what remained of the Lydiard estate on the market. Swindon Corporation had already expressed an interest in the mansion house and parkland, exclusive of the farms and pasture land.

The sale was conducted by auctioneers Fielder & Jones and took place at the Corn Hall, Cattle Market, Swindon on Thursday 29 July, 1943. There were ten lots comprising 'the Mansion House, Pleasure and Park Lands, Windmill Leaze Farm, Creeches Farm, Several Holdings of Arable and Pasture Land and several cottages and allotments.'

Lot 9 included the mansion together with gardens, ornamental lawns, stabling, adjacent pasture and woodlands and comprised about 58 acres. The park land measured 89 acres, the whole totalling just over 147 acres. The mansion was described as containing 41 rooms, an exquisite oak main staircase and some fine sculptured marble fireplaces. The sale catalogue went on to state that 'the walls, main ceilings and floors are in a good state of structural repair' although 'the roof and some of the secondary floors and ceilings are in need of repair', which may have been somewhat of an understatement, as the house was virtually derelict by then.

Cllr Francis Akers, a local businessman who lived in Moredon, Swindon bought all nine lots for £14,250. He offered the house and parkland to the Corporation for £4,500, the price he had paid for it. The Corporation paid a deposit of £450 on 11 August, 1943 with the balance due on 29 September, 1943. In the middle of wartime financial constraints this was a bold initiative.

Within weeks of the sale David Murray John, Swindon's visionary Town Clerk, had begun to get the restoration fund-raising ball rolling and John E.M. Macgregor, Technical Adviser on behalf of the Society for the Protection of Ancient Buildings reported in a document dated September 1943:

> That a building so rich in charm and grace should in two generations have degenerated and disintegrated to this extent while Swindon nearby was enjoying unprecedented prosperity, is a reflection indeed upon the material lust of the industrial revolution of the last century.

The Corporation's investment made during the middle of the Second World War was an audacious one but the Lydiard Estate soon began to play a part in the war effort. More than 40 acres of parkland were requisitioned by the War Department on what is today known as the events field near the Hook Street entrance.

A military camp built on the site was converted into the American 302nd Station Hospital in preparation to accept casualties from the 101st Airborne Division following the Normandy D-Day landings. Then in August 1944 the hospital was re-designated as a Prisoner of War Hospital. The third phase of the military camp began in 1945 when it became 160 POW Camp where German prisoners of war were accommodated, working on local farms while they waited to be repatriated at the end of the war.

But this was not the end of the Nissen huts. The buildings were converted to create 126 homes for local families and others bombed out of London. The first residents arrived in 1950 and the work was completed a year later. A small community was soon established on the edge of the parkland. Josie Holford, former Head of School at Poughkeepsie Day School, New York, who grew up in 'the huts' as they were fondly known, remembered gangs of workers arriving to work on the estate. 'It was totally overgrown. Workers, I assume they were displaced Poles, were brought in by lorry and deployed to do basic park upkeep and forestry.'

By 1960 most of the families had been rehoused in the newly built Penhill estate in Swindon. But even that wasn't the end of the Nissen huts, which were sold and reappeared as sheds in local gardens.

The special architectural and historical value of Lydiard House was officially recognised in 1955 when it was awarded a Grade I listing and added to what is now known as the National Heritage List of England. This scheme had begun as a Victorian initiative to protect ancient monuments and evolved into 'Salvage Lists', a record of historically important buildings damaged by bombing during the Second World War. This was the year in which the house opened to the public. Lord Lansdowne of Bowood House loaned items to furnish the State Rooms and conducted the official opening ceremony.

In 1958 a five-year plan was agreed between Swindon Corporation and the Ministry of Works to complete the restoration of Lydiard House. The Ministry contributed £2,600 annually and the Corporation £1,000. The Swindon Corporation Act 1947 stated that the mansion house was to be used as a conference centre and by 1962 Murray John was looking at how the whole estate could be better utilised by the general public.

In a letter to the Chairman and members of the Development Sub-Committee, Murray John wrote: 'The importance and value of the estate to the town have become recognised and its potentialities realised. The time seems opportune to complete the work and make the estate fully available for the use and enjoyment of the people of Swindon.'

In this same letter Murray John proposed the restoration of the lake, a project that would not be achieved for another forty years. He considered that: 'The scenic quality of the estate would thereby be greatly enhanced. In addition, the lake would have great practical advantages for the further education activities which it is hoped will take place at the estate.' Murray John envisaged a lake that could be used for fishing, canoeing and rowing. Swimming, however was ruled out as the stream that fed into the lake also ran through farmland and was polluted. Instead, Murray John proposed 'a small pre-fabricated open-air pool' at an estimated cost of £1,700.

Day conferences and meetings were already being held but one of the most successful ventures by far had been hostel accommodation for young people in the old stable block and it was considered this could be developed to create a centre for further education.

Murray John confirmed that the State Rooms on the ground floor of Lydiard House would remain separate from any development to the proposed Conference Centre as they were 'of outstanding beauty and must be kept open for the public.'

The house had received little maintenance following the 18th-century remodelling and throughout the late 19th and early 20th century it existed in a state of benign neglect. By the time Swindon Corporation took over the repair job was pretty extensive. Mr Flack, the Deputy Borough Architect, reported that 'the whole roof was held in place by its own weight, the friction between the tiles and spiders' webs.' The roof and floor joists were infested with woodworm and death-watch beetle while wet and dry rot had damaged the walls.

In 2004 a landscape restoration project began at Lydiard, the most extensive body of work undertaken since the acquisition of the house and park more than 60 years previously. The park landscape and walled garden were restored to their 18th-century splendour in a £5.3 million restoration project funded by the National Heritage Lottery Fund and supported by English Heritage and Natural England in partnership with local businesses including RWE npower, the BMW Group and Intel UK Ltd.

A team from Wessex Archaeology and more than 200 local volunteers conducted surveys across the park and made discoveries from the mundane (a garden shed) to features which enhance the known history of the estate. What was first thought to be a boat house on the edge of the lake turned out to be a 19th-century plunge pool built in about 1820 for George Richard St. John, 3rd Viscount Bolingbroke.

On the edge of the modern estate today overlooked by Lydiard Park Academy, archaeologists discovered evidence of a medieval park pale, a shallow, sunken ditch which retained deer within the royal parkland for hunting purposes.

The Walled Garden, which had lain fallow for more than fifty years, was excavated. Archaeologists discovered a well and a stone cistern and were able to plot the 18th-century paths and flower beds ready for replanting.

The coach house and stable block where Frederick St. John, 2nd Viscount Bolingbroke accommodated his many horses, was converted into a Tea Room with additional space for events.

Central to the project was the restoration of the lake. The lake or New Canal was lost in the early part of the 20th century when the dam wall was breached. During the ensuing 90 years the area became a wooded wilderness with self-seeded saplings and bushy undergrowth. When plans for the proposed restoration of the lake were made public, local residents at first mourned the loss of the wilderness playground. However, today it is difficult to imagine the park without the beautifully restored lake.

The earlier Lydiard ladies would not recognise the Palladian mansion house standing high in the north Wiltshire countryside, but for most the church of St. Mary's would be very familiar.

Visitors to the historic church in Lydiard Park often mistakenly think it is a private chapel. Although just a hop, skip and a jump from the back door of Lydiard House, St Mary's has always been a parish church. The house and church were once separated by a road, the route of which can still be followed along the hollow way to the probable site of the medieval village of Lydiard Tregoze. At first a small, cell like building and subsequently enlarged, a place of worship has stood on the site for more than one thousand years. Sir Simon Jenkins, journalist and former chair of the National Trust, wrote about St Mary's in his book *England's Thousand Best Churches*. He said of the contents of the south chapel 'were it to be removed lock stock and barrel to the Victoria and Albert Museum in London it would cause a national sensation.'

A view of St Mary's Church taken from the hollow way, the former thoroughfare from the medieval village of Lydiard Tregoze to the parish church.

The South Porch was added in the 15th century and indicates a period of prosperity in the local community when churches were extended and refurbished. It was here that the first part of the marriage and christening services took place and where women were 'churched' after giving birth. It was also a place where 'sinners' could stand and ask for the prayers of the congregation in an act of public penance.

One of the most significant changes made to the church environment occurred when George Richard, 3rd Viscount Bolingbroke returned to Lydiard in 1806 after a long sojourn in America.

Firstly, he wanted to put some distance between the parishioners who passed by the mansion house on their way to church. Next, he wanted to stop burials taking place on the south side of the church and close to his property, which he said rendered 'Lydiard House almost uninhabitable.' Following more than a year of negotiation with the ecclesiastical authorities Lord Bolingbroke was given permission to make the alterations.

Lord Bolingbroke paid for the building of a new rectory and a stable block close to the church for the parishioners' use while at worship and most importantly he received the peace and privacy he desired. The South Porch was closed and from 1812 until the present day those attending services at St Mary's have entered the church through the west door.

The oldest monument in the church is that of Nicholas and Elizabeth St. John at prayer, erected in 1592 by their son Sir John. However, by 1615 their grandson, Sir John St. John, 1st Baronet had begun his ambitious project of family memorials, the first of which was the St. John polyptych.

The polyptych was custom made for the north wall of the chancel of St Mary's and measures almost 15 feet (4.5 metres) high to the top of the pediment and 14 feet (4.2 metres) wide, including the lateral doors. Unlike a triptych, which consists of three parts, this extraordinary 17th-century construction has two pairs of hinged doors and multiple panels. The folding panels show the ancestry of the St. John family, beginning with Margaret Beauchamp who married Oliver St. John in about 1425.

The central panel consists of a family portrait, featuring Sir John St. John, 1st Baronet, along with his wife Anne, his parents Sir John and Lucy St. John, and his six sisters. The portrait was painted on canvas, most probably in London, and it is believed it was then rolled up for despatch to Lydiard House, where it was glued to one-inch-thick oak panels, which in turn were secured to two-inch-thick elm boards.

By 1683 the family decided the genealogical information needed updating, and repairs became necessary. The central doors were badly warped, and newly hinged outer doors were added. Further additions to the family tree were made in the 18th century, most probably by Henry, Viscount St. John (1652-1742), who had a special fondness for the Lydiard Park estate and spent a considerable amount of time there.

The complicated arrangement of 15 panels was constructed over a period of at least ten years, but it was not until the 1980s, when conservators Pauline Plummer, Joe Dawes and John Green began a major restoration project, that the masterpiece revealed more of its secrets, including a genealogical table that had been hidden since 1694.

The portrait had suffered from considerable overpainting and as Pauline Plummer FSA and Fellow of the International Institute for the Conservation of Historic and Artistic Works, stripped back the centuries of varnish, dirt and DIY, she discovered a painting of the finest quality, produced by an artist at the peak of his career. She suggested the artist might even have been William Larkin who painted portraits of members of the court of James I, an idea supported by eminent art historian Sir Roy Strong.

In 1633 Sir John St. John, 1st Baronet refitted the south aisle to accommodate another magnificent memorial erected in 1634. The eight-poster tomb depicts Sir John, his two wives and the thirteen children he had by his first wife Anne Leighton. The children still living at the time of the construction of the monument are seen kneeling, five sons at the head of their parents and three daughters at their feet. The four children who

The effigy of Anne Leighton on the St. John tomb in St. Mary's Church. Anne the first wife of Sir John St. John 1st Bt is depicted holding her 13th child.

had previously died are portrayed on the base. The spectacular alabaster, limestone and clunch monument was made in London, dismantled and transported to Lydiard Tregoze, no mean feat on 17th-century roads. When it was reassembled on arrival it proved to be too tall for the allocated space. Unfortunately, the monument has no sculptor's signature.

Above the door in the south chapel stands a memorial to Katherine Mompesson, the eldest sister of Sir John. Married to the disreputable Sir Giles Mompesson, Lady Katherine died in 1633. The monument was erected by Sir Giles and depicts the couple seated opposite each other. He is dressed in armour and holds an opened book; a helmet stands at his feet while Lady Katherine rests her left hand on a skull. Art historian Katharine Esdaile described the monument in her work *English Church Monuments 1510-1840* as 'that first of English Conversation Pieces, the enchanting Mompesson monument at Lydiard Tregoze' and Nikolaus Pevsner thought it 'a delightful piece, full of pensive melancholy.'

Situated in the chancel is the magnificent Golden Cavalier monument, a memorial to Captain Edward St. John, the last of the memorials commissioned by Sir John. Edward was the third of Sir John's sons to die fighting for the Royalist cause in the English Civil Wars, but Edward was the only one to receive such an extravagant memorial. Edward was fatally wounded at the 2nd Battle of Newbury in 1644. He was brought home to Lydiard where he died from his wounds four and a half months later. It is believed that the face and the uncovered hand of the figure were originally painted in natural colours and there is evidence of black paint beneath the gold. Records indicate that the monument was already 'gilt' by 1780.

The glorious 17th-century East window is the work of Abraham van Linge and was commissioned by Sir John St. John in about 1630. Abraham and his brother Bernard came to England from Emden, Friesland in around 1623. Examples of Abraham's work can be seen in the V&A, Lincoln College, Oxford, Queen's College, Oxford and Christ Church Cathedral, Oxford or, closer to home, in the Blue Closet in Lydiard House. A central olive tree supports heraldic references to the descent of the manor of Lydiard from the Ewyas family to the St. Johns. The two figures represent St John the Evangelist and St John the Baptist.

At the opposite end of the church the vibrant West window, erected in 1859 to the memory of local farmer John King by his two sisters Ann and Mary isn't to everyone's taste. Architectural historian Nikolaus Pevsner described the window as 'Large figures, strident colours, bad.'

In the 15th century the church was resplendent with wall paintings to instruct the illiterate congregation. Above the nave is a portrayal of the Martyrdom of St. Thomas Becket alongside another of St. Michael the Archangel weighing souls while an unusual 16th-century depiction of Christ's accusers at his Crucifixion looks down from the chancel arch. Throughout the church remnants of wall painting are evident, some merely decorative, some instructional text, and even some ghostly faces still waiting to be rediscovered.

And in a church with so many eye-popping features, the fragments of 15th-century glass could easily be overlooked. Executed by long forgotten itinerant Flemish glass workers, these stories in coloured glass reveal yet more history. It is said that when the glass workers arrived at a church to undertake a commission, they cast their eye around the local villagers for models to sit for their work, choosing those with strong and particularly beautiful features. What a thought that as we gaze up at these works of art the residents of medieval Lydiard Tregoze are looking down on us.

The intricately carved St. John family pew where the Lydiard Ladies worshipped, is Jacobean, and once faced the two-decker pulpit that stood against the north wall of the nave. A seating plan of the church dating from the 19th century reveals the pews used by the tenant farming families. Farmers from Midgehall, Spittleborough and Flaxlands were among those who occupied the north aisle. The tenants at the home farm then called Windmill Leaze, used one of the pews to the left of the nave aisle while farmers from Mannington, Toothill and Creeches occupied pews to the right.

The amazing fixtures and fittings of the church have required attention throughout the centuries but by far the most extensive conservation project in the history of the church was launched in 2011, supported by the National Heritage Lottery Fund and with a £100,000 financial pledge from the Friends of Lydiard Park. An English Heritage Place of Worship grant followed in 2012 and work to make the building weatherproof began in 2013.

A team headed by world renowned conservators Jane Rutherfoord and Eddie Sinclair made some exciting and unexpected discoveries during the long project. In the South Porch the team discovered a rare Christ Crown of Thorns 16th-century wall painting with a Renaissance style representation of the face of Christ and while working on the carved wooden corbels high in the church roof came the revelation that these had once been brightly coloured. The two corbels above the chancel arch have been repainted using techniques employed in the day. But perhaps the most surprising discovery was made when two 18th-century plaques were removed to ascertain how much of the wall painting remained intact behind them. Conservators were astounded to discover an ornamental niche, destroyed during iconoclastic damage in the 16th century. Amongst the rubble in the blocked-up niche was hidden a piece of the head of the statue that had once stood there.

The St. John Jacobean family pew, the wall paintings that appeared and disappeared as religious conflict came and went, all these features would have been familiar to the various Ladies of Lydiard as they too came and went.

2

The Early Ladies

THERE HAVE BEEN ladies at Lydiard, running busy households and raising their families, from time immemorial, but who was the first lady to live at Lydiard Park?

In 2004 an archaeological excavation made in advance of a £5 million landscape restoration project, discovered pieces of high-quality Roman building material in the area of the present-day car park close to the church of St Mary's.

The remains of 2nd- to 4th-century Romano-British pottery sites had already been discovered across the West Swindon area during excavations ahead of the proposed 1980s housing development. The conclusion reached by Wessex Archaeology was that the foundation course of a Roman building found in Lydiard Park contained reused material from a high-status building, possibly a villa. Sadly, it is impossible to discover any information about the woman whose home overlooked the Romano-British countryside. What a story that would be.

In a history spanning a thousand years, the Lydiard estate has belonged to just a handful of owners – the Ewyas, Tregoze, Grandison, Beauchamp and St. John families – one continuous blood line with six women inheriting the property.

The royal links that thread through the combined family histories date back to the 11th century to Harold of Ewyas, son of Ralph who was the nephew of King Edward the Confessor. Harold acquired numerous estates, among them the manor of Lydiard. It passed through three generations of the Ewyas family until it was inherited by Sybil, quite possibly the first Lady of Lydiard, if you don't count the Roman woman.

There are an awful lot of Sybils involved in the early story of Lydiard, and unfortunately no evidence as to whether they ever lived on the estate or just counted it among their landholdings and inheritance.

There is, however, a tantalising amount of information available about another Sybil (also called Sibilla), who married Robert Tregoz. Sybil was the daughter of Robert fitzHarold Ewyas and his wife Petronella and was born at Ewyas Harold, Herefordshire. She inherited the honor of Ewyas including Lydiard when her father died in 1198. Robert was the grandson of William de Tregoz, a wealthy French nobleman who held land on both sides of the channel. Robert was a supporter of Henry 'the Young King' son of Henry II and later was a steward in the household of King Richard 'the Lionheart.' He served as constable of Salisbury and Sheriff of Wiltshire and had established himself worthy of marrying the Wiltshire heiress Sybil Ewyas. Robert did very nicely out of his marriage, accumulating land in Herefordshire, Hampshire, Somerset, Surrey and Wiltshire.

Researching the marriage of Sybil and Robert Tregoz has proved challenging as there are conflicting accounts of how many husbands she had and in which order she married them. It seems most likely that she married Robert Tregoz in 1194.

Robert followed Richard I to Normandy and the Rev A.T. Bannister, Vicar of Ewias [Ewyas] Harold wrote in his account of the History of Ewias Harold that Robert never returned. King Richard died in 1199 when Bannister loses track of Robert, suggesting he may have died while in Normandy.

But Bruce Coplestone-Crow, writing in the Friends of Lydiard Tregoz Report 29 published in 1996, traces him to a period of service for King John in Normandy after this date. Perhaps he wasn't lost at all, just mislaid. By 1205 Robert was back in England where he died sometime in 1214.

Sybil quickly remarried after Robert's death and outlived her second husband Roger Clifford. Bannister goes on to say: 'She seems to have been a strong and masterful woman, executing deeds in her own name and ruling Ewias – and her three husbands

– with a firm, vigorous hand.'

Sybil had at least three children by Robert Tregoz who survived childhood. Her eldest son John died young and her third son William took holy orders. But it was her middle son, also named Robert, who put Lydiard on the map.

Between 1241 and 1258 Robert received three grants of oaks from the royal forest at Braydon, which suggests he was probably engaged in a building project at Lydiard. But what was he building – a permanent residence, or possibly a hunting lodge for entertaining? Robert was killed in the Second Barons' War fighting alongside Simon de Montfort at the Battle of Evesham. But the work at Lydiard continued and in 1270 Henry III granted the family a royal licence to impark woodland in order to create a deer park with gifts of numerous deer to replenish the stock.

Robert's wife, Juliana Cantilupe, the daughter of William de Cantilupe, survived her husband by twenty years. In old age Juliana wrote an account of their ancestry for her brother Sir Thomas Cantilupe, Bishop of Hereford. Written in Norman-French, Juliana traces their family history back to the French King Louis VIII. Sadly, she doesn't mention anything about her more recent past and where she lived with Robert during their marriage. The Cantilupe castle was at Foy in Herefordshire. Nothing is left today, but St Mary's Church, Foy has records of Juliana and a curved head on the arch of the northwest window is said to be in her image.

In 1271 Robert and Juliana's son John Tregoz was granted for life the right to hunt with his own dogs the hare, fox, badger, and cat in the royal forests of Wiltshire, Hampshire, Gloucestershire, Somerset and Oxfordshire, adding credence to the theory that the earliest property at Lydiard could have possibly been a hunting lodge.

By 1300 Robert and Juliana's granddaughter, Sibillia had inherited the Lydiard estate, which then descended to the Grandison family under some pretty turbulent conditions. The so called Despenser War (1321-22) was a revolt by the barons against the influence Hugh le Despenser and his son (also named

Hugh) exerted over King Edward II. Despenser the elder was an administrator and courtier and chief adviser to Edward II and along with his son was hated and feared in equal measure. Although defeated in the war, the Despenser father and son duo managed to emerge victorious and back in favour with the King to dominate the political scene for the next four years.

The war touched the Lydiard fortunes when Sibillia and William Grandison's son Peter was taken prisoner after the Battle of Boroughbridge. In 1323 Sibillia and William were forced to convey the manor of Lydiard to the medieval baddy Hugh le Despenser the elder in exchange for the release of their son.

When the Despensers' end came it was brutal and grisly. The good news is that Lydiard was restored to Sibillia and William and stayed in the Grandison family for another twenty years when Peter Grandison granted the reversion of the manor to his sister Sybil and her husband Roger de Beauchamp.

Lady Margaret Beauchamp, Duchess of Somerset

THE BEAUCHAMP FAMILY would own the manor of Lydiard for more than 90 years and at last we arrive at a Lydiard Lady about whom there is plenty of information, and even a portrait – Margaret Beauchamp.

Margaret Beauchamp was born in around 1409, the daughter of Sir John Beauchamp and his second wife Edith Stourton. Margaret's father, Sir John Beauchamp, died in 1412 when his estate passed first to his wife for her lifetime with his son John as his heir. However, John junior died in 1420 before reaching his majority when Lydiard and the various other Beauchamp properties descended to eleven-year-old Margaret.

It is not known exactly when Margaret Beauchamp married Sir Oliver St. John, nor the date of birth of the first of their seven children, and Sir Oliver St. John's own birthplace remains unknown. He was born in 1398 most probably at Paulerspury in Northamptonshire, but some records say he was born at Penmarc Castle or possibly Fonmon Castle, two of the St. John family homes in Glamorganshire. He died in France on March 4, 1437, most probably during fighting following the execution of Joan of Arc when the English were driven out of France. He was buried in the Church of St Jacques des Jacobins in Rouen. This church was demolished in 1793 and any monument to Sir Oliver has been lost.

Margaret was left a very desirable, wealthy widow of about 28 years old, but she didn't rush into a second marriage and it is fair to assume that she played an active part in the choice of her second husband. In about 1442 she married John Beaufort, Duke of Somerset and in 1443 she gave birth to a daughter named Margaret.

Beaufort descended from an illegitimate son of John of Gaunt (son of Edward III). His military career began at the age of fifteen but any glory he achieved was eclipsed by his ignominious later years. John Beaufort fought in Henry V's French campaign and in 1421 served alongside his stepfather Thomas, Duke of Clarence in Anjou. Clarence was killed at the Battle of Bauge where John and his younger brother Edmund were taken prisoner. Despite several attempts at negotiation John remained incarcerated for seventeen years until his release in 1438 having paid a ransom that financially wiped him out. By then in failing health, his prospects as a husband were less than desirable. But perhaps Margaret could see the bigger picture and his royal connections compensated for his lack of fortune.

John Beaufort continued in the service of the King. However, following a disastrous expedition at the end of what would later be known as the Hundred Years' War, he returned disgraced and was banished from court, retreating to his Wimborne estate where he died on 27 May, 1444; the rumour was he had committed suicide.

On 14 April, 1447 Margaret married for the third and last time. Her husband was Lionel 6th Lord Welles by whom she had a son John. Lord Welles was killed in the Yorkist victory at the Battle of Towton in 1461 during the Wars of the Roses. Margaret's son John married Cecily of York a daughter of Edward VI. Cecily's sister Elizabeth married Henry VII, Margaret's grandson.

In 1445 and 1458 conveyances were made of Beauchamp held manors at Lydiard and Bletsoe and secured for Margaret's two sons by Oliver St. John. Her elder son Sir John St. John headed the senior branch of the family at Bletsoe while second son Oliver inherited the manor of Lydiard in Wiltshire.

Evidence suggests that Margaret Beauchamp was a strong-willed and astute woman, carefully preserving and overseeing her considerable legacy. Following the death of her second husband she received a grant for life of £166 13s 4d annually. Manors in Somerset, Essex, Northamptonshire, Lincolnshire, Dorset and Devon, acquired during her husband's lifetime, were transferred to her by royal licence.

Margaret died in the summer of 1482 aged about 73. She was buried beside her second husband John Beaufort in Wimborne Minster, Dorset. The effigy of the couple on their tomb features them clasping their right hands.

More than two hundred years later, when Sir John St. John, 1st Baronet, commissioned the St. John polyptych, a portrait of Margaret Beauchamp was installed on the pediment of the monument. It is not known from where the artist sought his inspiration, perhaps in 1615 there was a portrait of Margaret still in existence.

Lady Margaret Beaufort, Countess of Richmond and Derby

FOR SOME OF the women in this book there is little information; maybe just a birth year, a marriage and a death date. Some are mentioned in the correspondence of their contemporaries, others leave letters of their own and for one Lydiard lady there is a wealth of information. Lady Margaret Beaufort's legacy lasts to this day from the two Cambridge colleges she founded to her descendants in the modern royal family.

In 2011 the Woodvilles, a group of historical re-enactors, set up camp at Lydiard Park. For one weekend that summer they brought the 15th-century way of life, weapons and warfare to the elegant parkland, giving local people a time travel taste of the Wars of the Roses period. All very fitting as one of the early

Lydiard ladies played a crucial role in this dynastic drama, uniting her St. John kin with the victor, Henry VII.

Margaret Beaufort was born on 31 May, 1443, the only living child of Margaret Beauchamp's second marriage to John Beaufort, Duke of Somerset. The complicated Beaufort family history is the stuff of a modern-day soap opera. John Beaufort and his siblings were descended from the illegitimate son of John of Gaunt (the son of Edward III) and his mistress Katherine Swynford. Following the marriage of their parents, the Beaufort children were later legitimised by the Pope and by a Statute of Richard II. Although they remained close to the throne they were later excluded from the succession by Henry IV.

Margaret was little more than a year old when her father died. She was raised by her mother and grew up alongside her seven St. John half siblings, brothers John and Oliver and sisters Elizabeth, Margaret, Agnes, Mary and Edith. The family divided their time between Bletsoe Castle in Bedfordshire and Maxey Castle, a fortified manor house, near the village of Maxey, Peterborough.

After her father's death Henry VI granted the wardship and marriage of the young Margaret to his favourite William de la Pole, earl (later duke) of Suffolk who promptly married her off to his son John. Like most marriages arranged during childhood, Margaret remained living with her mother. The marriage was annulled after Suffolk's downfall and execution in 1450 and in 1455 Henry VI placed Margaret under the wardship of his two half-brothers Edmund and Jasper Tudor.

The twelve year old Margaret was soon married for a second time and her husband, 26-year-old Edmund Tudor, more than twice her age, was not prepared to wait to consummate the marriage. He was anxious to produce a son to secure his right to his young wife's considerable wealth, but died of plague before the child was born.

Margaret's son was born at Pembroke Castle on 28 January, 1457. The birth was traumatic and both psychologically and physically damaging. Margaret would never have another child. Aged thirteen she was a mother and a widow and within months she would marry again, but this would be a marriage to a man of her own choice. With no influence at the time of her first two marriages, Margaret made sure any subsequent alliances would be with a man of her own choosing. From here on in Margaret would not be pushed around. Any decisions she made would be hers and hers alone. She became a force to be reckoned with.

At just fourteen years old she negotiated a marriage with Sir Henry Stafford, a shrewd move as he seamlessly shifted allegiance from Lancaster to York, managing to protect Margaret, her son and her wealth.

In 1455 a civil war kicked off that would rumble on and off for thirty years. Four hundred years later it was christened the Wars of the Roses by Sir Walter Scott in his 19th-century novel *Anne of Geierstein*. More recently historical novelist Philippa Gregory has renamed it the Cousins' War. But at the time the protagonists were probably too busy fighting to call it anything other than 'bloody', and Margaret Beaufort was placed centre stage by her Lancastrian roots. But why was Margaret so critical to the future of the Beaufort family? By 1471 she was the last living member descended from the male line of that dynasty. In fact, she was as (if not more) worthy of gaining the contested crown than her son Henry Tudor, but of course as a woman her claim would have been dismissed.

In 1462 the recently proclaimed Yorkist king Edward IV granted wardship of Margaret's five year old son to William, Lord Herbert and the boy moved in with the Herbert family at Raglan Castle in Monmouthshire. Herbert was captured and executed following the Battle of Edgcote in 1469 and Margaret regained some control over her twelve year old son. When another reshuffle of monarchs put the boy in danger, Henry's uncle Jasper took him into exile in Brittany and out of harm's way.

For more than twenty years Margaret saw little of her son; her driving force was to keep them both alive and to navigate the dangers and political turmoil of the civil war.

Following Stafford's death in 1471 Margaret married

Thomas Stanley, Earl of Derby despite having taken a vow of perpetual chastity. Not yet 30, Margaret was a desirable marriage prospect and this alliance was one of political strategy. Stanley owned vast tracts of land in Lancashire, Cheshire and north Wales and was also steward in the household of Edward IV. From this influential position in the Yorkist court Margaret began to negotiate her son's return to England with the King and a marriage with one of Edward's daughters by Elizabeth Woodville.

In 1483 the failed Buckingham Rebellion in which Margaret had been complicit placed her in a perilous situation. She lost her property and was placed under virtual house arrest.

Then in 1485 Henry made his bid for the throne. He landed at Milford Haven, West Wales on 7 August, 1485 with his uncle Jasper and some 3,000 men including 1,500 troops from the European low country and a number of Scottish mercenaries. From here he led his small army through the Welsh Marches to the Midlands, his numbers increasing as he progressed, but it was still an uneven contest with Richard's army an estimated 12,000 strong. The events of the battle are still argued and contested today; even the site of the battleground itself is disputed. And on the bloody battlefield the crown continued to be at the mercy of political manoeuvring. The Stanley family (Margaret's husband Lord Thomas Stanley and his younger brother Sir William) hedged their bets, their eventual support of Henry proving to be Richard's downfall. The King was hacked down, his crown seized and placed on Henry's head by Lord Stanley on the battlefield.

With the accession to the throne of her son, Lady Margaret enjoyed an unprecedented level of political power and freedom. Margaret behaved and acted as if she were Queen, styling herself the King's Mother. How Elizabeth of York, Henry's wife, felt about all this remains a matter for conjecture.

A grotesque, a fantastic or mythical figure, looks down on the churchyard from above the South Chapel.

Margaret owned an extensive portfolio of properties located in Devon, Dorset and stretching across the country into Yorkshire. To these she later added personal acquisitions and crown property. The magnificent Collyweston Palace in Northamptonshire was given to her by her son in 1486. Believed to have equalled Hampton Court Palace in its heyday, Collyweston was where Margaret based herself as administrator for the Midlands on behalf of her son.

Margaret was well educated and well read, who understood both French and Latin. She was pious yet politically savvy. Was she controlling and domineering? – most probably. Her life's work had been to protect her son. A driven, determined and sometimes ruthless woman, her household accounts reveal her more frivolous side. She was a woman who loved clothes and entertaining and, perhaps surprisingly, gambling.

Was she devious? Well, no one played by the rulebook in the Medieval period. Was there even a Medieval rulebook? Was she a murderer? Modern day Ricardians, those followers who want to absolve Richard III of the murder of the two young Princes in the Tower, have put Margaret in the frame.

Margaret died on 29 June, 1509, just two weeks after the coronation of her grandson Henry VIII. She was 66 years of age and had outlived her son by two months.

Her detailed and lengthy will, dated 6 January, 1508, was not proved until three years after her death. As might be expected, Margaret gave considerable thought to the repose of her soul, her burial place and memorial and unsurprisingly she wished to lie close to her son in the chapel of Henry the seventh at Westminster.

She left detailed instructions for the services to take place after her death in her own private chapel and also in the church of the parish in which she died and the fifteen neighbouring parishes as well as every parish through which her funeral cortege should pass. She also gave instructions for a service to be held in all the churches where her body should rest overnight on the way to Westminster Abbey.

As it happened Margaret's body didn't have to travel very far at all as she died at the Abbot of Westminster's house. Her body was moved from Cheyneygates where she had been staying following the coronation of her grandson Henry VIII, to the Abbey Refectory before burial on 9 July. On the top of the black marble altar monument lies a gilt bronze effigy of Margaret by the Italian sculptor Pietro Torrigiano. The lifelike face was probably modelled on her death mask and depicts Margaret in old age, her hands together in prayer and wearing a widow's dress with a hood and long mantle.

A translation of the Latin inscription by Erasmus reads:

Margaret of Richmond, mother of Henry VII, grandmother of Henry VIII, who gave a salary to three monks of this convent and founded a grammar school at Wimborne, and to a preacher throughout England, and to two interpreters of Scripture, one at Oxford, the other at Cambridge, where she likewise founded two colleges, one to Christ, and the other to St John, his disciple. Died A.D.1509, III Kalends of July [29 June].

The bequests in her will were many and included directions that her household should be kept together for a quarter of a year, and her old and serviceable household servants were to be rewarded at the discretion of her executors, among whom were John Fisher, Bishop of Rochester, Charles Somerset, Lord Herbert the king's chamberlain and Sir John St. John her chamberlain.

She left her large collection of devotional books to be divided between Christ's and St John's, the two Cambridge colleges she founded along with items from her private chapel including hangings, vestments, altar clothes, plate and jewels not already the subject of other bequests.

To 'Sir John Seynt John our chamberlain' she left 'a stonding cupp gilt with a couer' (most probably a chalice). To her nephew John Saynt John, she left various gilt bowls and a lot of bedding, including a featherbed, a bolster, pillows and sheets. This kinsman also received 'a book of velom of Canterbury tales in Englische.'

To 'the Quene of Scottes' (her granddaughter) she left 'a gyrdell of gold conteyning xxix lynkes with a grete pomaunder at oon ende' ponder' and to 'the queen' 'a girdill of gold conteyning vj flowers and xxxvj linkes, with a grett cnopp ate on ende and a hoke on the other ende, all ponder' (Elizabeth of York was dead by the time Margaret wrote her will in 1508 and Katherine of Aragon, Henry VIII's first wife yet to be crowned Queen).

John Fisher, Bishop of Rochester, who joined Margaret's household in 1494, became her spiritual advisor and following her death executor of her will. It is from his writings that we gain a picture of Margaret and his account of her life in the *Mornynge Remembraunce* is full of affectionate praise.

All Englonde for her dethe had cause of wepynge. The poore Creatures that were wonte to receive her Almes, to whome she was always pyteous and mercyfull; the Studyentes of both the Unyversytees, to whome she was a Moder; all the Learned Men of Englonde, to whome she was a veray Patroness; all the vertuous and devoute persones, to whom she was a lovynge Syster; all the good relygyous Men and Women, whome she so often was wonted to vysyte and comforte; all good Preests and Clercks, to whome she was a true defendresse; all the Noblemen and Women, to whome she was a Myrroure and Exampler of honoure; all the comyn people of this Realme, for whome she was in theyr causes a comyn Medyatryce, and toke right grete displeasure for them; and generally the hole Realme hath cause to complayne and to morne her dethe …

It has to be remembered that this probably wasn't an unbiased account. John Fisher was not only a personal friend but he was talking about the new King Henry VIII's grandmother.

The National Portrait Gallery holds two portraits of Margaret, the earlier by an unknown artist dates from the second half of the 17th century. There are also several mezzotint and stipple engravings in the NPG collection, the earliest dated 1714 and a model of the Westminster Abbey effigy. All the portraits depict Margaret at her devotions and all bear a marked similarity to a painting held at St John's College, Cambridge. This portrait was commissioned by Margaret's spiritual advisor, John Fisher Bishop of Rochester shortly after her death and was painted by Dutch artist Meynnart Wewyck. The painting was first held at the Bishop of Rochester's palace in Lambeth Marsh but following Henry VIII's Act of Supremacy in 1534 and the subsequent dissolution of the monasteries was later removed to St John's for safe keeping. Recent dendrochronology tests on the picture frame have dated it to before 1521, which corresponds with an acquisition entry in the college archives of 1534.

Everything Margaret Beaufort accomplished in her life was motivated firstly by her love of God and her son, then for her family; the Lady Margaret effect upon the St. Johns was phenomenal. During her lifetime she brought them positions at court and influential marriages. Her nephew John acted as her chamberlain and executor of her will. His son, another John St. John, was knighted by Henry VII and the inscription on his monument in St Mary's, Bletsoe reads that he was the foster child of the Countess of Richmond and brought up from his earliest years for the service of princes. Her half-brother Oliver was a member of her riding household and his son John was also employed in her household.

The St. Johns would celebrate their Tudor connections in perpetuity. Almost two hundred years later when John St John, 1st Baronet commissioned the genealogical St. John polyptych, a whole panel was devoted to their shared Tudor lineage.

Elizabeth Blount

WHEN NICHOLAS ST. JOHN was born in 1523 Henry VIII was still a popular King, still happily married to Katherine of Aragon, still confident of producing a male heir. Nicholas was the son of John St. John and his first wife Margaret Carew. He served as MP for Camelford and Saltash in Cornwall, and closer to home in Cricklade, Great Bedwyn and Marlborough. Nicholas enjoyed a lively political career and has been described as both quarrelsome and litigious. Of course, there is far more information available about Nicholas than there is about Elizabeth.

It is difficult to pin down the dates of Elizabeth's life events other than her death, which is recorded on the monument in St Mary's. She died on 11 August, 1587, but when she was born or the date of her marriage to Nicholas remains unknown. The couple had eight children and their heir John was born in 1552. It is probably fair to hazard a guess that the marriage took place between 1548-1550 when Elizabeth was aged between 15-20.

Elizabeth was the daughter of Sir Richard Blount and his wife Elizabeth Lyster, daughter of the Lord Chief Justice. Sir Richard served as a Gentleman of the Chamber to Henry VIII and as a Gentleman of the Privy chamber during the young Edward

This sixteenth century monument in St. Mary's Church is of Elizabeth Blount at prayer with her husband Nicholas St. John.

VI's reign. He was returned as MP for Steyning in 1553 and was made Lord Lieutenant of Oxfordshire in 1559-61. Sir Richard also served as Lieutenant of the Tower of London between 1559-61. He was buried in the Tower church of St Peter ad Vincula and a large monument in the Sanctuary commemorates both Sir Richard and his son Sir Michael Blount who also served as Lieutenant of the Tower.

Elizabeth's grandfather Sir Richard Blount of Iver, Sheriff of Buckinghamshire and Bedfordshire, purchased the Manor of Mapledurham Gurney, Oxfordshire in 1490 and it was here that Elizabeth grew up with her two brothers, Michael and Richard and a sister Barbara. An inventory included in Dame Elizabeth Blounte's (Elizabeth's mother) will reveals a sizeable property with a parlour, hall, buttery, kitchen and several first-floor chambers. Outbuildings included a cheesehouse, bakehouse, brewhouse and milkhouse and it is likely the property was a moated manor house. The Old Manor House on the banks of the River Thames is today a Grade II* listed property. Investigations in the 1980s identified evidence of a boundary ditch or possibly a filled in moat. During their marriage Elizabeth and Nicholas St. John spent much of their time at Mapledurham and it is likely that their children were born and baptised there.

The much grander neighbouring Mapledurham House was built following Michael Blount's (Elizabeth's brother) purchase of the neighbouring manor of Mapledurham Chazey, creating an estate of around 2,800 acres. Building work began shortly before Michael's death and was completed in 1612 by his son Richard.

The best historical resource for personal details of a family during this period are wills and Elizabeth's name is mentioned in those of both her parents.

Elizabeth and Nicholas and their children received the following bequests in her father's will.

> To my sonne Saintion I give the best gelding that I have. To my daughter his Wife I give one Ring of fine golde, weing thurtie shillings, and to every one of theire children one Ringe of fine golde weing twentie shillings.

The St. John family also received numerous bequests in Elizabeth's mother's will. Elizabeth was to receive her mother's best velvet gown, a black enamelled tablet of gold, and a cup of silver and gilt.

> Item I doe gyve and bequeathe unto John St John sonne and heire apparent of Nicholas St John a pott or cupp of silver and guilte of the valewe of sixe poundes thirtene shillinges fower pence, to be bought for him by my executoure hereafter named after my decease.
>
> And my will is that if anye of the saide Elenor St John Dorothie St John or Jane St John shall happen to decease before the tyme of her marriage or before her age of Fower and twentye yeares that her legacie before herein given whiche shall happen so to decease shalbe equallye devided amongst her other sisters whiche shall then survive.

> And further I doe give and bequeathe unto Oliver St
> John Richard St John sonnes of the saide Nicholas St John,
> and unto Richarde Sherley sonne of Franncis Sherleye esquire
> deceased, to everie of theme a peece of silver plate of the valewe
> of fortie shillinges a peece or else forty shillinges in lawfull
> englishe monneye to everie of theme as theire choyses, to be
> paide within one quarter of a yeare next after my decease.

Before Sir John St. John, 1st Baronet began commissioning the stupendous 17th-century family memorials, the Nicholas and Elizabeth St. John monument was the star attraction in St Mary's Church. Erected by their son John in 1592 the monument now stands next to a window in the south aisle, but this was not its original position. It is thought to have once stood either on the south side of the chancel or in the old South Chapel. The couple are depicted kneeling side by side beneath an elaborately painted canopy although it is believed that the achievement on the top was not part of the original design. In 1886 the Bristol firm of Joseph Bell & Sons undertook a number of decorating jobs in the church, including the 'renovation and decoration of Monuments of Lord Bolingbroke's Family'. This included the complete repainting of the memorial to Nicholas and Elizabeth St. John monument.

The monument measures 3.3 metres high; 1.5 metres wide; 1 metre deep and the kneeling figures of Nicholas and Elizabeth measure 1.1 metres high.

The Latin translation reads:

> Here lie (good reader) buried in the hope of the blessed
> resurrection the bodies of Nicholas St John, armiger, and of
> his wife, Elizabeth: he was for the reigns of King Edward,
> Queen Mary, and Queen Elizabeth of the number of the
> chosen retinue (commonly called pensioners) and died while
> holding that rank with the sovereign. Elizabeth his wife was
> the daughter of Richard Blunt, Knight, and by her had three
> sons and five daughters: John, Oliver, Richard, Elizabeth,

Catherine, Eleanor, Dorothea, and Jane. John his eldest son took to wife the daughter of Walter Hungerford, Knight. Oliver and Richard are still alive, unmarried. Elizabeth his eldest daughter married St George of the County of Cambridge, Catherine (married) Webb, Eleanor (married) Cave of the County of Northampton, Dorothea (married) Egiocke of (the County of Warwick, Jane (married) Nicolas of the County of Wiltshire. Nicholas St John himself departed this life on the eighth day of November, 1589, and Elizabeth his wife departed this life on the eleventh day of August in the year of our Lord 1587, leaving a noteworthy trophy to those who followed her of unsullied repute and wholesome life. John St John their son set up this monument out of affection to those good parents who had served him so well. In the year of our Lord, 1592.

In life and in death Christ is our riches
Thou who dost hope for the happy span of a long life,
They hope deceives thee, we both bear witness.

Elizabeth's eldest daughter Elizabeth married Sir Richard St George, a member of the College of Arms. Appointed as Norroy King of Arms in 1603 and later as Clarenceux, the second highest heraldic appointment in England, Sir Richard assisted his nephew Sir John St. John 1st Baronet in the compilation of genealogical information on the St. John polyptych.

3

The Good Life

Lucy Hungerford, Lady St. John

A N ACCOUNT OF the life and times of Lucy Hungerford has to include a mention of an all-important royal visit when Queen Elizabeth called in at Lydiard.

The Queen was on one of her regular progresses, a time when she travelled the country with a large retinue of servants, relatives, courtiers and hangers on. The purpose was twofold; firstly, to give the people an opportunity to see their sovereign monarch and also to allow her residences to have a thorough clean. A 16th-century deep clean involved clearing out the garderobes, the medieval toilet.

The Queen left Nonsuch Palace in Surrey on 8 August, 1592, arriving at Bisham in Berkshire on 13 August and Newbury on the 26 August. She reached Wiltshire during the last week in August and was at Ramsbury on the 28 arriving at nearby Liddington the following day.

It is likely the Queen spent the night of 31 August at Lydiard House, although this raises the question of where her vast retinue stayed. It has been suggested portable accommodation such as tents and pavilions travelled with the court and could have been erected in the grounds. The Privy Council met at Lydiard House on 1 September and before the Queen took her leave, she knighted her kinsman John St. John. The two were third cousins once removed, tracing their ancestry back to Margaret Beauchamp. By 10 October she was back at Hampton Court Palace, stopping off at Down Ampney, Sudeley Castle and Rycote in Oxfordshire on the way home.

Lucy Hungerford, wife of Sir John St. John Kt.

We can only imagine how much preparation this whirlwind visit caused poor Lucy, John St. John's wife, and how much money the whole event cost them. That same year the Queen visited Sir Henry Lee at Ditchley Park. Sir Henry commissioned a portrait of the Queen known as the Ditchley Portrait but famously declined a second visit as the first one had nearly bankrupted him.

Lucy Hungerford was born in around 1560, the eldest of Sir Walter and his second wife Anne Dormer's four children. The Hungerford men were a volatile bunch. Lucy's grandfather Walter, First Baron Hungerford of Heytesbury, was attainted by act of parliament in 1540. A former squire of the body to Henry VIII, he was charged with an involvement in various seditious plots against the King and also with 'committing unnatural offences.' He was beheaded at Tower Hill on 28 July, 1540 gaining the dubious distinction of being the first person to be executed under the Buggery Act of 1533. Sir Thomas Cromwell, Henry's favourite henchman, lost his head that same day.

Lucy's parents were a far from happily married couple. In 1570 her father, another Sir Walter, sued his wife for divorce accusing her of adultery and trying to poison him. Anne was acquitted but Walter was a sore loser and refused to pay his legal costs, which saw him incarcerated in the Fleet prison. Anne settled in Belgium where she petitioned for her children, concerned that her vengeful husband would disinherit them. Following the death of his son, Walter left his property to his brother Sir Edward with remainder to his sons by his mistress.

In contrast Lucy Hungerford appeared to enjoy a happy marriage with her husband John St. John. The couple married at St Mary the Virgin, Black Bourton, Oxfordshire on 29 October, 1582 and went on to have ten children, seven daughters and three sons. Following John's death in 1594. Lucy quickly remarried a distant cousin, Sir Anthony Hungerford and gave birth to three more children, bringing her combined family up to a count of thirteen. Lucy died on 4 June, 1598 and is buried with her first husband, John St. John, in the family vault at St Mary's, Lydiard Tregoze.

Her eldest son Sir John St. John, 1st Baronet, supported the Royalist cause during the English Civil Wars in which three of his sons were killed. Sir Edward Hungerford, her son by her second marriage, was on the opposing side and commanded the local forces of Wiltshire Parliamentarians in 1642-45.

A portrait of Lucy, painted in the English School style in *c.*1590 when she was about thirty years old, hangs above the doors in the Drawing Room in Lydiard House. In 2002 Janet Backhouse, a former curator of Illuminated Manuscripts at the British Library, examined the portrait anew. She described Lucy's dress as rich but comparatively sombre and typical of that worn by a landed lady of her time. Lucy wears a baroque pendant in the shape of a mermaid and holds a feather fan. Janet Backhouse drew particular attention to the girdle book bound in gold and decorated in black enamel hanging on a gold chain about Lucy's waist. These 16th-century devotional girdle books were designed to be portable and were highly desirable and the height of fashion.

The six St. John sisters from left to right Lucy, Barbara, Eleanor, Jane, Anne and Katherine. Detail from the 17th century polyptych in St. Mary's Church.

In 1615 John St John 1st Baronet, Lucy's son, took delivery of a family memorial and at its centre was a portrait like no other. John and his wife are pictured standing left of the portrait; he is dressed in a fine suit of half Greenwich armour and Anne in the latest fashion. Central to the portrait are John's parents, Sir John St. John and his wife Lucy kneeling on a sarcophagus. On the right of the portrait are John's six sisters standing in order of seniority. Eldest sister Katherine stands closest to the viewer and Lucy the youngest closest to her parents. The portrait is an idealised view of the family, gathered around their devout parents.

When the painting was completed in 1615 John had been dead for 21 years and Lucy for more than fifteen.

Following the death of John and Lucy the St. John children were dispersed; the two sons were made wards of court, the unmarried daughters placed in the care of their Uncle Oliver St. John at Battersea.

Katherine St. John, Lady Mompesson

ELDEST DAUGHTER KATHERINE is believed to have been born around 1584 and with her siblings spent her early childhood at the medieval mansion in Lydiard Park. Following their father's death in 1594 Katherine's two brothers Walter and John were made Wards of Court. Although Lucy quickly remarried it appears that not all her children remained with her. Some of the girls at least were sent to live at Battersea with their uncle Oliver St John – a pretty unhappy time for them according to Katherine's niece Lucy Hutchinson.

Katherine married Giles Mompesson in 1606/7 at St John's Church, Hackney. Katherine could have been as young as 13 although this would not have been considered exceptionally young – her sister-in-law Anne Leighton was this age when she married Katherine's brother John at the same church eighteen months previously.

Life at Battersea might not have been a barrel of laughs but I'd wager a purse full of gold and silver thread that it was preferable to living with Sir Giles. In 1621 he was described as 'a litle black man of a black swart complection with a litle black beard' but perhaps after eighteen years of marriage Katherine had stopped noticing – there were far more pressing problems for her to cope with by then.

The St. John family, along with most other aristocrats of the day, were quick to exploit their advantages and Sir Giles had one hugely influential in-law. Katherine's sister Barbara was married to Sir Edward Villiers, half-brother to royal favourite George Villiers, 1st Duke of Buckingham, who was close to the ear of King James I.

Through Buckingham Sir Giles managed to land a few plum positions. Knighted in 1616, by 1620 Sir Giles had been appointed Commissioner to grant Licences to Keepers of Inns and Alehouses, a hugely lucrative job if you knew how to play it. The entrepreneurial Sir Giles was avaricious and a miscreant, accused of accepting bribes and threatening and bullying behaviour. He charged exorbitant fees of the inn and alehouse keepers and those that couldn't afford to pay up he prosecuted, approximately 4,000 people. But that wasn't all. He also obtained the patent for the decayed timber on the Crown Estates, intended for the Navy but which Sir Giles sold for his own profit. He then went on to procure the patent and exclusive right to manufacture gold and silver thread, a process that was incredibly dangerous. Wiltshire antiquarian John Aubrey records those involved in the production suffered badly – 'they rotted their heads and arms and brought lameness on those that wrought it, some losing their eyes and many their lives by the venom of the vapours that came from it.'

Mompesson's misuse of this perk caused such an uproar that the King called in the patent, but it was Mompesson's abuse of his role as Alehouse Commissioner that really got him into trouble. Sir Giles was stripped of his knighthood, fined £10,000 and sentenced to life imprisonment. However, he had already done a flit overseas by the time the judgement came in so his sentence was commuted to perpetual banishment. The general opinion was that James came down so heavily on Sir Giles to appease a people that hated the royal favourite. George Villiers, an extremely unpopular figure, was eventually stabbed to death in a Portsmouth pub on 23 August, 1628 by Army Officer John Felton.

Although he was a thoroughly disreputable character, Katherine continued to support her husband and in 1623 submitted a petition requesting permission for him to return home to attend to his affairs. The fine paid by Sir Giles was returned to her in a roundabout way. The King granted that the £10,000 be placed in the hands of Katherine's brother Sir John St. John and her younger half-brother Edward Hungerford 'in trust to the use of Lady Mompesson and her child.' Wily Sir Giles lay low in France where Katherine joined him, returning to England when all the fuss had died down.

This mention of a child in the King's grant to Katherine is the only reference to any surviving children born to the couple. When her sister-in-law Anne Leighton died in 1628 following the birth of her 13th child, Katherine took in the baby, a boy named Henry, until Sir John remarried in 1630.

Following Katherine's death Sir Giles erected an extravagant monument to her memory which today is positioned above the door to the St. John chapel. He describes Katherine as being 'peerless in beautry, chastity, constancy, piety, and every form of virtue.' His intention was that when he died his 'ashes' should be laid with Katherine. Unfortunately, the parish registers for 1633, when Katherine died, and 1663, when Giles died, have not survived.

Anne St. John, Lady Ayliffe

NEXT TO KATHERINE stands Anne St. John, the second sister born in around 1585. Anne married local boy Sir George Ayliffe on 2 November, 1610 and moved just up the road to Grittenham in the parish of Brinkworth.

Sir George's ancestor, Royal surgeon Sir John Ayliffe, was gifted the Manor of Grittenham and lands in Grittenham and Braydon, with Grittenham Mill by a grateful Henry VIII in 1541. The Ayliffe family lived in the manor house until the middle of the 19th century. By the end of that century the house was said to be in a ruinous condition and was subsequently demolished.

Sadly, there is little to be discovered about the life of Anne Ayliffe, born at a time when the main requirement of a wife was to be fertile. We know she was certainly this as Anne had at least twelve children. The couple's eldest son John was born in 1611, another son, born in 1617, was named St. John after Anne's family. The couple's youngest daughter was named Apsley in honour of Anne's brother-in-law, Sir Allen Apsley married to her youngest sister Lucy.

Anne died in *c.*1629 and when Sir George made his will in 1640, he stated that he wished to be buried in the St. John family vault at St Mary's alongside his wife. He died in December 1643 and his helmet with the oak tree crest is mounted high in the roof of St Mary's, the only remaining piece of his armour, probably brought into church on the occasion of his funeral. The couple's youngest daughter Apsley was buried with her parents just three days after Sir George's funeral. Their eldest son John died two years later and along with another daughter, Frances, were buried in the St. John vault. Anne's hatchment, a diamond shaped painting of the Ayliffe family coat of arms, hangs in St Michael's and All Angel's Church, Brinkworth.

Anne's eldest daughter, also named Anne, married another local boy Sir Edward Hyde of Purton who later became the Earl of Clarendon and Lord Chancellor. Pregnant Anne caught smallpox and suffered a miscarriage, dying just six months after the wedding. Although this marriage was sadly a short one, Edward featured in the St. John history for many years. He was a good friend and advisor to Anne, Countess of Rochester, but disapproved of another St. John lady, Barbara Castlemaine, Charles II's notorious mistress.

Sir George and Lady Anne's daughter Deborah Ayliffe married her first cousin John St. John, son of the first Baronet. John was one of three brothers who died fighting for the Royalist cause in the English Civil Wars. Captain John served in Sir Jacob Astley's Regiment of Foot and was mortally wounded during the blockade of the Royalist Garrison at Newark in late 1643. He was buried on 15 December 1643 in the chancel of the parish church of Newark according to his instructions.

Jane St. John, Lady Pleydell

THE MIDGEHALL PEW in St Mary's Church, Lydiard Tregoze, at the east end of the north, Clarendon aisle dates from the 17th century and was commissioned by the Pleydell family. The story goes that the Pleydell ladies complained that a raised ridge on the back of the pew damaged their dresses and it was later removed. The same story exists about the Windmill Leaze pew, perhaps the church furniture proved a nuisance for all the fashionable ladies of Lydiard Tregoze.

In the middle of the 12th century Midgehall was granted as a grange or manor to Stanley Abbey, a sort of country house cum farm complete with moat, by Henry, Duke of Normandy, subsequently Henry II. All rather grand for a place whose name means *'a corner or nook of land infested by midges.'*

Canny Coleshill farmer William Pleydell had foreseen the demise of the monastic domains and had staked his claim on Midgehall before Henry VIII actually got the party started. In 1534 William obtained a 95-year lease from the Abbot of Stanley and he made sure he jolly well hung on to it. In 1606 the property belonged to William's great grandson, Charles Pleydell, the second husband of Jane St. John.

Jane St. John was born in around 1586, the third of Sir John St. John and his wife Lucy Hungerford's six surviving daughters. Her first husband was Sir Robert Atye of Kilburn Priory, Middlesex whom she married on 22 May, 1606 at St. Margaret's, Westminster. Robert Atye's father was Arthur Atye, Principal of St Alban Hall and Orator of the University of Oxford and a former secretary to Robert Dudley, Earl of Leicester. His mother, Judith Hungerford, was a member of Lucy Hungerford's (Jane's mother) extended family. It was easy to see that this was an advantageous match and one from which Jane's brother, Sir John St. John 1st Baronet, benefited financially. The couple went on to have two children, Arthur born 1606/7, who died before attaining his inheritance, and Eleanor born in 1608.

Robert died in 1612 and in 1615 Jane returned to Lydiard Tregoze where she married widower Charles Pleydell at St. Mary's Church on 14 October.

So how did Jane occupy her days in that corner or nook of land infested by midges? Perhaps not surprisingly Jane and Charles returned to her home at Kilburn Priory where they had at least ten children (possibly twelve) most of them baptised at the church of St. John, Hampstead. Today Kilburn straddles the

London Borough of Camden to the east and Brent to the west, but before the Reformation it was a place of pilgrimage, taking its name from Kilburn Priory, a small monastic community of nuns established in the 12th century.

Charles was knighted in 1620 and thereafter described himself as Sir Charles Pleydell of Midgehall, Wiltshire and Kilburn Priory. He served as high sheriff for the County of Wiltshire and Alderman and Mayor of Wootton Bassett. Charles died in 1642 and was buried at St. Mary's, Lydiard Tregoze, but what became of Jane? Did she return to Midgehall to eventually join him in death at St. Mary's? It seems more likely she remained at her house in Kilburn. When Jane died in 1654, she was buried in the churchyard at St. Mary's, Willesden, probably on the instructions of her eldest daughter Eleanor Atye married to Sir William Roberts who owned considerable land in the area.

The Pleydell memorial in St Mary's Church was erected by one of Jane's stepsons and memorialises both his mother Katharine and Jane and the 19 children they had between them.

The Pleydell monument stands above the door to the South Porch of St. Mary's Church and commemorates the two families of Sir Charles Pleydell.

Eleanor, Lady St. John

ELEANOR ST JOHN was born in around 1587, the fourth of the six sisters, and is pictured third from the left standing between Barbara and Jane in the family portrait.

Eleanor married Sir William St. John at St Mary's, Battersea on February 10, 1611/12. William was born around 1585 at Uchelola (High Light) one of the St. John's homes in Glamorgan. The couple were distant cousins, both descending from the sons of John St. John and his wife Isabel. Eleanor was the 4x great granddaughter of Oliver St. John and Margaret Beauchamp while William was the 3x great grandson of Alexander John St. John and his wife Margery.

Sir William was a naval officer and captained various ships in the King's navy. In December 1622 the French and Spanish ambassadors claimed that a ship called the *Croissant* carrying 100,000 crowns of grain of French merchants and sums of ready money had been taken under the eyes of two of King James I's ships, the *Adventure* and the *Garland*. The *Adventure* was under the command of Sir William St. John, thus implicating him in a case of piracy. He was briefly imprisoned and lost command of his ship.

It seems likely that Eleanor spent a great deal of her marriage separated from her husband. Perhaps Eleanor and her children lived with her uncle and aunt in the manor house on the Thames during William's long sea voyages. Two of her children were both baptised in the church there; Howard on 3 December, 1612 and a daughter Anne on 5 February, 1613.

William died in 1641 and was buried with an infant daughter in St Mary's Church, Battersea. The couple's son Howard died a year later. Eleanor lived on for another six years when she too was buried in St Mary's on 20 July, 1648.

Barbara St. John, Lady Villiers

BARBARA ST. JOHN, Lady Villiers signed her will on 3 September, 1672. Just thirteen days later she was buried in the north ambulatory near St Paul's Chapel in Westminster Abbey.

Barbara had lived through the reign of four monarchs and a Lord Protector. She had seen the union of the English & Scottish crowns and the failure of the Gunpowder Plot, the devastation of

Barbara St. John, sister of Sir John St. John 1st Bt and wife of Sir Edward Villiers.

the English Civil Wars, the beheading of Charles I, the institution of the Commonwealth and the Restoration Settlement. She had married into one of the most influential families of the age and had been at the centre of court life for more than sixty years, yet surprisingly little is known about the woman herself.

Barbara was born in around 1588, probably at Lydiard House, the 5th daughter of Sir John St. John and his wife Lucy. She married Edward Villiers in 1611 in what might not have appeared at first as a particular advantageous liaison. That is until

Edward's half-brother George caught the eye of King James and rapidly secured the position of King's favourite. George was made first a Knight of the Garter, then Viscount Villiers, and eventually Duke of Buckingham and he took his Villiers and St. John family with him on his rapid ascent at the court of King James.

Sir Edward Villiers was another disreputable character. The first blot on his reputation came when he was involved in a scandal involving regimental funds when he was a Captain in the Leicestershire militia. After the rise to fame of his half-brother George, Sir Edward's ambitions knew no bounds and his influence politically and at court soared. First, he was knighted, then in 1616 given the lucrative post of Master of the Mint. In 1618 he was made Comptroller of the Wards and in 1620 Ambassador to Munster and MP for Westminster. His mercurial good fortune saw him temporarily flee the country in 1621, embroiled in controversy concerning a patent for the licensing of gold and silver thread along with his brother-in-law, Sir Giles Mompesson.

In 1623 Barbara's childhood guardian Sir Oliver St. John was created Viscount Grandison of Limerick and with no sons to succeed him Sir Oliver's title went to his niece Barbara by special remainder and subsequently to her eldest son William and his two younger brothers in turn.

But what of Barbara the woman? There was little she hadn't seen or coped with during her long life. Her eldest son William, 2nd Viscount Grandison, was wounded at the siege of Bristol on 26 July, 1643 and died the following month at Oxford. Her youngest son Edward was wounded at the 1st Battle of Newbury in 1643 but recovered and like Barbara, lived to see the restoration of the monarchy.

And her daughter Eleanor, a maid of honour at Queen Henrietta Maria's court, spent time in the Tower of London in 1633 following her affair with the Queen's favourite Henry Jermyn. The Villiers family called upon the King to force Jermyn to marry the pregnant girl and both were sent to the Tower where Eleanor admitted there had been no promise of marriage between them.

How did others see Barbara? George Ayliffe, her sister Anne's husband, left a bequest in his will to her calling her 'my dearest and best friend that ever I found in the world, my Ladie Villiers, my dearest sister, £20 for a diamond ring, in memorie of me her poor brother, who ever truly loved her and honoured her even to death ...'

Sir Edward Villiers died on 7 September, 1626 at his official residence in the college of Youghal and was buried at St. Mary's, Youghal in County Cork, Ireland. The inscription on his grave slab describes him as the Lord President of Munster.

Widowed in 1626 while still in her 30s, Barbara never remarried. Although financially burdened by her husband's untimely death and the ensuing debts she was left to pay, Barbara appeared to do quite nicely. Fourteen years after Edward's death details of her pension in 1640 revealed she received £1,122 8s 10d, two pence in the pound weight of all silver coins minted in the Tower of London, one of the perks of being the widow of a former Master of the Mint, and by the 1660s she also received some financial support from the Crown.

When the time came to make her will she left her money and possessions to her family, friends, and her servants. Her maid Alice Barrett received £30 and the pick of her wardrobe. Her servant George was left £40 while Thomas Smith, a footman received £15 and all in her employ took home a Quarter's wages over and above. To the poor of the parish where she died, she left £3 and to the poor of the parish where she was buried, she left £5.

To her granddaughter Barbara, Duchess of Castlemaine, the mistress of Charles II, she left a ring and to 'my deare Grandchild Charles Earle of Southampton,' one of the children of this union, she left 'a Ring of the value of Twenty pounds to be paid to him when he arriveth att the age of Twelve yeare.'

Barbara left her unmarried daughter Eleanor, disgraced as a young woman by Henry Jermyn, £250 a year plus an equal share of the remains of the estate after all the bequests had been paid. Eleanor was appointed as one of the executors of her mother's will along with her brothers George, Viscount Grandison and Edward Villiers.

Barbara's portrait painted *c.*1630, hangs above the state bed in the State Bedroom at Lydiard House while Sir Edward's portrait by Gortzius Geldorp is in the Dining Room.

Lucy St. John, Lady Apsley

THE YOUNGEST SISTER is Lucy born in 1589 and just five years old at the time of her father's death. Lucy is the sister about whom we know most, thanks to her daughter Lucy Hutchinson.

Lucy Hutchinson wrote an account of the life of her husband Colonel Hutchinson, one of the 59 Commissioners who signed the death warrant of Charles I. In her manuscript she also included a short autobiography in which she writes about her mother and the St. John sisters. 'There were not in those days so many beautifull women found in any famely as these.'

Life wasn't easy for the sisters. Still a young child when her parents died, Lucy St. John was shipped off to Battersea and their Uncle Oliver, but it wasn't the uncle who was the problem. Lucy Hutchinson writes:

> …she was carried to be brought up in the house of the Lord Grandison, her father's younger brother, an honorable and excellent person, but married to a lady so jealous of him, and so ill-natured in her jealous fitts to any thing that was related to him, that her cruelties to my mother exceeded the stories of stepmothers.

The remaining sisters 'were disperst to severll places' until Sir John married Anne Leighton when they were reunited at Lydiard House.

By the time the family portrait at the centre of the polyptych was painted Lucy was the only unmarried sister. However, within months of the installation of the polyptych in St Mary's Church Lucy had married Sir Allen Apsley, Surveyor of Marine Victuals of the Royal Navy, at St Ann's, Blackfriars on 23 October, 1615.

Lucy St. John was Apsley's third wife and with him came several children that she happily embraced, before having eight of her own. Lucy Hutchinson describes her parents in rhapsodic terms, their marriage apparently idyllic, but of course she might have been a tiny bit biased.

In 1617 Apsley was appointed Lieutenant of the Tower of London and Lucy's new home became the Queen's House, built by Henry VIII for Anne Boleyn. Here Lucy became 'a mother to the prisoners' and with her generous allowance of £300 a year from Apsley supported the officer's widows and orphans and the scientific experiments long term resident Sir Walter Raleigh engaged in.

The Queen's House, Tower of London where Lucy St. John, Lady Apsley lived when her husband Sir Allen was Lieutenant of the Tower.

In 1628 Apsley accompanied the hated Royal favourite George Villiers, Duke of Buckingham, on the ill-fated Isle of Re expedition. As Lucy Hutchinson writes it was 'an ill-manag'd expedition to the Isle of Rhee, under pretence of helping them, [the Protestants] but so order'd that it prov'd the losse of Rochell, the strong fort and best defence of all the Protestants in France.' Apsley developed consumption on this expedition from which he never recovered. His wife nursed him during his illness, prolonging his life longer than his physicians had believed possible. He died in the Tower on 24 May, 1630 and was buried in the chapel of St Peter ad Vincula.

Apsley died mired in debt leaving Lucy and her children destitute. She made a hasty second marriage to Sir Leventhorpe Francke whose promises to help her proved false. The couple soon separated. In later life Lucy St. John lived with her daughter at the Hutchinson family home in Owthorpe, Nottinghamshire where she died in 1659 aged 70.

The sisters with their linked arms add a charming informality to this commemorative portrait full of symbolism and heraldic emblems and boasting of the family's famous antecedents and Royal connections. The women are all dressed in black, not in mourning for their deceased parents but as a symbol of the family's wealth – a good black cloth was expensive. They each wear a fashionable French hood of different styles and falling lace collars. The polyptych remains closed for most of the year but is opened on the Heritage Open Days and on other specific occasions.

Sadly, there is much more information about their husbands, than the women themselves, but thanks to Sir John this magnificent portrait of them survives.

Anne Leighton, Lady St. John

A NNE LEIGHTON GREW up during the volatile period of political intrigue and religious fervour that marked the end of the Tudor period and the beginning of the Stuart.

Anne was the daughter of professional soldier Sir Thomas Leighton and Elizabeth Knollys, and the Knollys family were about as close to Queen Elizabeth as it was possible to be. Anne's grandmother Katherine Knollys, the daughter of Mary Boleyn, was the Queen's first cousin. Rumour had it she might have

Anne Leighton, the first wife of Sir John St. John, 1st Bt.

even been her half-sister. There is a much-disputed theory that Katherine was the product of her mother's affair with Henry VIII. The King however, did not acknowledge Katherine as his daughter, but he did put a lot of opportunities and wealth in her way. Perhaps neither Mary nor the King could be entirely sure, but there is no denying that Katherine bore a strong resemblance to Henry.

Katherine served in the young Princess Elizabeth's household before she acceded to the throne and records reveal that Katherine and her husband Francis took part in the coronation ceremony and celebrations. From 1558 Katherine served as a Lady of the Bedchamber, accompanied by her daughters, including young Elizabeth Knollys then aged just 9 years old, who served as a Maid of the Chamber.

Elizabeth Knollys spent pretty much her whole life in the confines of the claustrophobic court where the women employed to care for the Queen's every need had to apply for a licence to be absent from court for more than two weeks. A position at court was all about status with the top posts reserved for ladies from the upper echelons of society.

In 1566 Elizabeth Knollys was one of the Gentlewomen of the Privy Chamber, the day room where the Queen spent much of her time. Elizabeth had daily access to the Queen, able to confide in her and to influence her, and it is known that she was involved in privy council business and decision making.

In 1578 Elizabeth Knollys married Sir Thomas Leighton; she was 28 and he was 43. They had three children that survived to adulthood, a son Thomas born *c*.1584 and two daughters, Elizabeth born in 1583 and Anne in 1591.

Anne was christened on 14 October, 1591 at the parish church of St Mary the Virgin, Hanbury. Four miles from Droitwich, Hanbury in Worcestershire was the Leighton family seat, although it is likely she spent a considerable amount of her childhood at court where her mother remained for most of her marriage to Leighton.

Anne's father Thomas had been a Gentleman of the Household for ten years, before which he had served as a soldier and had seen service at the Siege of Rouen in 1562 and in defence of the garrison at Le Havre a year later. In 1569 he had commanded 500 harquebusiers during the Northern Rebellion and in 1570 he was appointed Governor of Jersey and Guernsey. The association between the Leighton and St. John families was a long standing one.

When their father died in 1594 the St. John boys John and Walter were first made wards of a senior member of the Bletsoe branch of the St. John family. The wardship was later transferred to their uncle Sir Oliver St. John, Viscount Grandison.

Sadly, the Lydiard heir, Walter died in a bathing accident off the Island of Hermes while staying with the Leighton family. Following Walter's death, Queen Elizabeth granted Sir Thomas Leighton the wardship of the wealthy, young John St. John and lease of the St. John lands after an appeal from Lady Elizabeth Leighton who stated that she and her husband were 'minded to match him to their daughter.'

John matriculated at Trinity College, Oxford in 1601 and was admitted to Lincoln's Inn in the year of his marriage. He went on to become Member of Parliament for Wiltshire from 1624 to 1625 and served as High Sheriff of Wiltshire from 1632 to 1633.

Anne Leighton and John St. John were married at St John's Church, Hackney on 9 July, 1604. John was 19 years old and Anne 12. It is unlikely that they lived together as man and wife after the wedding, especially as their first child, a son Oliver, was not born until February 1612/13. However, Lucy Hutchinson, the daughter of Sir John's sister Lucy St. John suggests that the sisters returned to Lydiard House soon after John and Anne's marriage, writing in her Memoirs of Colonel Hutchinson. 'The rest of my aunts, my mother's sisters, were dispersed to several places, when they grew up till my uncle, Sir John St. John, being married to the daughter of Sir Thomas Laten, they were all again brought home to their brother's house.'

Lucy also writes of the kindness shown by Anne to her mother, the youngest of six sisters among whom there was considerable rivalry in the matrimonial stakes. 'My uncle's wife, who had a mother's kindnesse for her, persuaded her to remove herselfe from her sister's envie, by going along with her to the Isle of Jernsey where her father was governor.'

The St. John family was the largest landowner in the 17th-century parish of Lydiard Tregoze which included parkland, numerous farms and parcels of land in the neighbouring parish of Lydiard Millicent.

In 1604 the medieval mansion house that the newly married couple called home consisted of two wings linked by a central hall block. This was a period when a number of titled families were renovating their ancestral homes and, in many instances, it was the lady of the house who was in charge of building operations. Perhaps Anne was the driving force behind the modernisation of Lydiard House, dragging it out of the past and into the 17th century.

Unlike subsequent generations of the family who divided their time between their various properties, John and Anne chose Lydiard Park as their preferred home. These were busy times for the young couple and their growing family. The St. Johns had status, wealth and connections. The family finances were secure. These, it might be said, were the golden years.

A portrait of Anne thought to be by Gilbert Jackson hangs in the dining room at Lydiard House and bears a striking resemblance to the Tudor Queen. Dressed in fashions typical of the period, Anne wears a grey dress with epaulettes embroidered in green, red and gold and a deep lace collar edged with red and gold embroidery. Her hairstyle is typically Elizabethan worn swept back, with her hairline plucked to accentuate her forehead, and an inset pendant with earrings to match.

Anne also appears in the St. John polyptych in St Mary's Church commissioned by Sir John in 1615. Anne stands beside her husband to the left of the portrait, their arms interlinked in a display of informality and intimacy. Unfortunately, Anne's face has suffered from overpainting across the centuries and has lost the quality of others in the portrait.

Anne died on 19 September, 1628 soon after the birth of her 13th child. She is depicted on the magnificent alabaster St. John tomb in St Mary's church. The carving is of the highest quality and a comparison with existing portraits confirms the accuracy of the representations of Sir John and his two wives.

The inscription reads:

Anne was the daughter of Thomas Leighton, Knight, by his wife Elizabeth of the Knowles family and of the kindred of

Queen Elizabeth, as blessed in character as in connection. She
lived for thirty seven years, endowed with noble gifts of mind,
body, and manner, a rare example of virtue and piety; she was
the mother of thirteen surviving children, in the end, long worn
down by the painful agonies of her last confinement and at last
overcome, she fled to heaven on the 19th September, 1638.*

Anne did not live to see the turmoil of the Civil War in which
five of her sons played an active role. The first of her three sons to
die in the Royalist cause was William, born in 1617. William, a
lieutenant in the infantry, was killed in action fighting alongside
Prince Rupert at Cirencester in February 1642/3. His body was
returned to Lydiard House where he was buried alongside his
mother in the family vault in St Mary's.

Later the same year, John, Anne's second son, died fighting in
Nottinghamshire. The Royal garrison at Newark was blockaded
during the winter of 1643 and it is believed John was killed during
fierce fighting. He was buried in the chancel of the parish church
at Newark.

The third of Anne's sons to die fighting in the Royalist
ranks was Edward. A captain in Sir John Byron's Regiment of
Horse, Edward saw action at the second battle of Newbury on 27
October, 1644. Although fatally wounded he returned to Lydiard
House, eventually dying from his injuries more than five months
later. He was also buried in the family vault at St Mary's.

Anne's two youngest sons Walter and Henry both married
daughters of Cromwellian sympathiser Oliver St. John, Chief
Justice of the Common Pleas, nailing their colours firmly to the
Parliamentarian mast.

Margaret Whitmore, Lady Grobham

SIR JOHN REMAINED a widower for two years before
remarrying. His second wife, Lady Margaret St. John boasts
the distinction of appearing in effigy on two church monuments
– and that was before she was even dead.

*The date is incorrectly recorded and should read 1628.

Lady grobeham
Wicklow second
wife to the first
S.ʳ Iohn. S.ᵗ Iohn Bar.ᵗ

Margaret Whitmore, second wife of Sir John St. John, 1st Bt.

Margaret was born in around 1576, the daughter of Alderman William Whitmore, a member of the Worshipful Company of Haberdashers with business premises at 8 Lombard Street, traditionally the home of goldsmiths, moneylenders and merchants. Her mother was Anne, the daughter of Alderman William Bond, another rich merchant. Margaret was the middle child of nine siblings.

The Whitmore family definitely had its collective finger on the pulse of commercial enterprise and civic life in the City where both Margaret's elder brothers were also engaged in business. Margaret's second brother Sir George Whitmore, was another merchant and a local politician who served as Lord Mayor of London in 1631-2. An ardent royalist, Sir George raised money and troops for the royalist cause during the English Civil Wars and was imprisoned several times for his subversive activities.

Margaret's elder sister Elizabeth married Sir William Craven, Lord Mayor of London in 1610-1611, who was said to be the inspiration for the legend of Dick Whittington. It was reputed that when Elizabeth died in 1624, she was one of the wealthiest women in England. William and Elizabeth's son, William Craven 1st Earl of Craven, was the champion and protector (even husband according to rumour) of the widowed Elizabeth of Bohemia, the elder sister of Charles I. It was for her that he built Ashdown House in Oxfordshire, although sadly she died before it was completed. More than 50 years later Ashdown House provided a sanctuary for the attainted Henry St. John, Viscount Bolingbroke.

Margaret was in her late twenties when she first married. Her husband, Sir Richard Grobham, a wealthy, Wiltshire landowner, was more than 25 years her senior. The couple divided their time between their Wiltshire estate and a property in Chancery Lane, London. They were married for 27 years but apparently had no children, or certainly none that survived childhood.

The inscription on Sir Richard's ornate monument reads:

> In a vaute heere under lyeth the bodie of Sr Richard Grobham Knight who enjoyed a happie lyfe 78 yeares and having byn marryed to Margaret the daughter of William Whitmore of London Esquier 27 yeares depted this transitory lyfe the 5th daye of July 1629

The effigy of Sir Richard on his tomb in the parish church of St Giles in Great Wishford depicts him dressed in armour with his hands folded over the Bible; Margaret lies next to him dressed in plain widow's weeds.

In his will Sir Richard bequeaths:

And I doe give graunt, etc., that my good vertuous and loueinge wife the Lady Margarett Grobham, who hath truly deserved much more then I have or can give her, shall have to her own vse and disposeinge all such jewells, chaynes, buttons borders rings apparel and all other her ornaments for her person and all such coach [coach] horses and furniture for coach and coach horses as I shall have at the tyme of my death, and not by me otherwise disposed of.

He goes on to say: 'I appoint that my said wife shall presently or shortly after my decease have fower hundred pounds in money delivered to her for her then present necessary expenses and occasions ...'

Of course, it wasn't all straightforward and although Margaret was made an executor of the will along with various other Grobham/Howe family members, a dispute arose in 1637 concerning the administration of rents and profits of Sir Richard's lands in Wiltshire, Gloucestershire and Somerset.

Life was rather different for Margaret when she married Sir John St. John, as he had several surviving children. Three of Sir John's children had died in the intervening years between their mother's death and their father's remarriage. Nicholas and Elizabeth died within days of each other in April 1629 and Thomas who had died in July 1630. Sir John and Lady Margaret married on 23 October, 1630 at the Grobham family home in Great Wishford, near Salisbury, a forty-mile journey from Sir John's home at Lydiard Park.

The elder two St. John siblings married within a couple of years of their father; Oliver in 1634 and Anne in 1632. John and William would both fight for the King in the English Civil Wars, both dying in 1643. The younger children Barbara, Edward, Lucy, Walter, Francis and Henry divided their time between Bolingbroke House, Battersea, which their father had inherited from his uncle Oliver, Viscount Grandison, and Lydiard House.

Margaret was 54 years old, 10 years older than Sir John, when she took on the young St. John brood. Although she obviously didn't have the day-to-day hands-on care of the children, one assumes she did play a role in the nurturing of the youngsters.

A portrait of Margaret painted at the time of her marriage to Sir John hangs in the Dining Room at Lydiard House above one of Anne Leighton, her predecessor. Compared to the youthful Anne you might at first glance think that Margaret was, well quite frankly, no oil painting. However, an examination of Margaret's dress reveals a woman of great taste, dressed in the height of 17th-century fashion.

And, unlike his disreputable descendants, Sir John obviously knew a good woman when he saw one. When it came to leaving a lasting memorial, Margaret's place on his right-hand side was assured.

The magnificent alabaster St. John memorial in St Mary's Church was commissioned, executed and delivered fourteen years before Sir John's death. Margaret was also alive and kicking at the time, with four years left to run on her clock.

The effigy of Margaret Whitmore, Lady Grobham, Sir John St. John's second wife, lies on his right-hand side on the St. John tomb in St. Mary's Church.

The inscription Sir John dictated for the memorial honours his first wife and then goes on to mention his second:

> Margaret was the daughter of William Whitmore, Knight of Apley in the county of Shropshire; she is living, in her fifty eighth year, notable for the fame of her virtue and given to good works; she is to be added to the tomb of this family when her time comes unless she one day decided otherwise.

If any further evidence was needed as proof that Margaret was a 17th-century fashionista, look no further than the effigy on the St. John tomb. Margaret wears her hair fashionable curled at the sides and is dressed in a gown, which the exquisite craftmanship of the sculptor shows to great advantage. The dress features a bodice with scalloped tabs tied with a ribbon sash, a high neck and standing collar with ballooned and paned sleeves with double cuffs. But Margaret was more than just a fashion plate. In her left hand she holds a book, the pages held open by her index finger, indicating scholarly learning and religious devotion.

Margaret died in 1637 and was buried in the St. John family vault with Sir John's first wife Anne. Interred with them were William and Captain Edward St. John, killed in the Civil War, Oliver St. John who died in 1641 aged 28, three boys and a girl who died in childhood and Sir John himself who died in 1648.

4

War and Peace

Anne, Countess of Rochester

THE ST. JOHN's played a prominent role in the events of the English Civil Wars period. The men were close to the monarchy and the parliamentarians, supporting both sides at various times in the conflict; and the women, well they enjoyed intimacy and influence in equal measure.

Three fascinating 17th-century women with links to the Lydiard estate are Anne, Countess of Rochester, her sister-in-law Lady Johanna St. John and royal mistress Barbara, Countess of Castlemaine.

Anne was born on 5 November, 1614, the second child and eldest daughter of Sir John St. John 1st Baronet and his first wife Anne Leighton. Following her mother's death in 1628, fourteen-year-old Anne became the eldest female in her father's household. Was she expected to take control of the Lydiard estate? Unlikely but not impossible. Did she learn her management skills from her mother or was she placed in another establishment for instruction? Whoever taught her, she learned well and through her long life she practised diplomacy laced with cunning and made some useful contacts. She married twice and survived two periods of widowhood during the turbulent Civil Wars, the Interregnum and the Restoration. She emerged from this period with a controlling personality and an inability to keep out of the business of other family members.

A portrait of Anne hangs in Hatchlands Park, East Clandon near Guildford, Surrey. In the half-length portrait by Sir Peter Lely Anne boldly meets the gaze of the viewer, giving us a glimpse of her courage and audacity. She wears a low-cut black dress with pearls inset in the sleeves and pearl jewellery. Her hair is dressed in ringlets. It has to be said that Anne lacks the beauty of her mother, favouring her father's St. John features more with her long face and nose. Unfortunately, there are no portraits of Anne at Lydiard House. She does, however make an appearance on the spectacular St. John tomb in St Mary's Church, depicted kneeling at the feet of her parents.

The Lydiard House Anne St. John grew up in was in need of a bit of DIY. The Palladian makeover would not take place for more than a hundred years, but Anne's parents did stamp their mark on the Tudor property with extensions made to the medieval manor house. However, Anne wasn't over-fond of her father's Wiltshire estate and was said to consider it rather dull. Anne much preferred the home of her uncle Oliver St. John, 1st Viscount Grandison, who became Lord of the Manor of Battersea in 1625. By then Battersea was a fashionable area, providing a country retreat for the rich and famous making their fortune in the teeming City. It was from the manor house at Battersea that Anne married Sir Francis Henry Lee in the neighbouring parish church of St Mary's, on 2 October, 1632. However, the church in which Anne St. John and Francis Lee were married is not the one that stands today on the same site. In 1771 the medieval church, although altered and enlarged during its long history, was found to be no longer fit for purpose and was demolished. Stonemason and local resident Joseph Dixon built the new church with his brother Richard.

The Lee's were another well connected family. Francis's father Sir Henry Lee had inherited the Ditchley Park estate in Oxfordshire from his cousin, also named Sir Henry Lee. This Sir Henry Lee had been the Queen's Champion from 1559-90. Following his retirement in 1590 Sir Henry returned to Ditchley where he lived openly with his mistress Anne Vavasour, a liaison that had much displeased the Queen. In 1592 the Queen visited Ditchley Park as an act of forgiveness. The portrait by Marcus Gheeraerts painted to commemorate the visit includes symbolisms of forgiveness with the Queen depicted standing on a map of England, her feet firmly planted in Oxfordshire on the Ditchley estate.

At the time of their marriage Anne was 18 and Francis Henry Lee, the young 2nd Baronet of Quarrendon just 16. Although the union was a carefully brokered alliance the young couples' marriage was a happy one. In 1637 a son Henry was christened at the parish church on 18 December and the following year a second son Francis Henry was born. But in 1639 tragedy struck when Francis contracted smallpox. The parish registers at Spelsbury record that he was 'buryed the 23 of July and dyed at Ditchly ye same day.' He was 24 years old. During his final days he refused to see Anne for fear that she would also become ill. The following year a daughter Helena also died and was buried in the Lee family vault at Spelsbury.

The new decade heralded a parlous time in which to live in England, but Anne had all bases covered with her own Royal connections at Court and her Parliamentarian kinsman Oliver St. John, appointed Solicitor General in 1641 and Lord Chief Justice of the Common Pleas in 1648.

In widowhood Anne proved to be independent, determined and possessed of an iron will. She was in no hurry to remarry, in part influenced by a clause in Sir Francis Henry's will that would see her lose control of the Lee family properties if remarried. By 1644 this clause had been removed and the Lee estate released from sequestration with a £2,000 penalty. Anne decided the time was right to take a second husband and she certainly didn't settle for the stay-at-home type. Henry Wilmot was already an experienced soldier who had fought for Charles I in the Bishops' Wars. He was quick to pledge allegiance to the King at the outbreak of the First English Civil War, gaining Royal recognition following action at the Battle of Newcastle in 1640 and at Edgehill in 1642. Although unpopular with the King's nephew Prince Rupert who considered him lazy and arrogant, Henry became a great favourite of the King's son.

Propaganda and gossip circulated during these politically precarious times as Anne's clandestine existence continued. It has been stated that Anne and Wilmot spent most of their marriage apart and claims are made that they only met on a handful of occasions. When in April 1647 Anne gave birth to a son there were those who cast doubt on the child's father. Interrogating the parentage of John Wilmot (later 2nd Earl of Rochester) antiquary Anthony Wood wrote some years later: 'I have been credibly informed by knowing men that this John, Earl of Rochester, was begotten by Sir Allen Apsley' and that Anne was 'notorious for her salaciousness.'

In the tradition of her fiercely Royalist family Anne discreetly supported the King's cause throughout the war, hiding Edward Hyde at Ditchley when he was forced to flee the Royalist headquarters at Oxford in 1642 and providing horses for his escape while supplying arms to the King's men at the Battle of Edgehill. But her commitment would go much further.

By 1649 the King was dead but the fight was not over. Cromwell sought redress against enemies of the regime and to reward supporters with a redistribution of royalist wealth. The Interregnum was an unstable period of espionage and counter intelligence and Anne was immersed in the intrigue.

Following defeat at the Battle of Worcester in 1651, Wilmot led Charles II to safety and into exile. Anne joined her husband in France where other members of the loyal St. John family continued to work for the royalist cause. Her cousin Edward Villiers, son of her aunt Barbara St. John and Sir Edward Villiers, was one of the founders of the Sealed Knot, a secret committee formed to support a royalist uprising and the restoration of the monarchy, active between 1653-59. Anne had friends and relatives in high places and she used her influence every which way she could passing sensitive information between the exiled court and Royalist sympathisers at home. Edward Hyde, Earl of Clarendon and Lord Chancellor whose first wife was Anne's cousin, proved a loyal, lifelong friend, as did Sir Ralph Verney of Claydon, an old friend of the Wilmot family.

Henry died in exile in February 1658 and was buried in Bruges. It is said that his body was exhumed after the Restoration and brought back to England where it was reinterred in the Lee family vault at Spelsbury.

Once again Anne was a widow trying to protect her inheritance for her family, determined to hang onto both the Lee and the Wilmot estates for the sake of her three sons. She would eventually manage to rescue her estate from Parliamentarian sequestration but sadly in 1659 her son Henry Lee, died and in 1667 her second son Francis Lee also died. Now she fought to protect their inheritance for her grandchildren. It has been suggested that Anne had a closer relationship with her Lee sons and favoured her Lee granddaughters, but there is challenging evidence to this theory in surviving documents, including Anne's letters and her will.

Anne continued to use her influence at court and through her cousin Barbara, Lady Castlemaine, managed to secure the king's favour on a match between her son John Wilmot and wealthy heiress Elizabeth Mallet, complete with a favourable marriage settlement despite the couple's impulsive elopement.

The notorious John Wilmot, 2nd Earl of Rochester continues to fascinate historians. Was he as debauched and corrupt as we are led to believe? Was all the pornographic literature attributed to him actually penned by him? Some eminent academics think otherwise and a manuscript of his poem 'Upon Nothing' held at the National Archives surprisingly contains amendments made in Anne's own hand. Whether these alterations were made under instruction by John or made by her after his death cannot be determined.

Anne's relationship with Rochester was a tortured one but there can be no denying Anne's depth of feeling for her son, especially in his dying weeks. Ravaged by illness variously attributed to syphilis and alcoholism Rochester returned to his home at High Lodge, Woodstock Park in April 1680 where he was described as being in a state of collapse. During the months of June and July 1680 Anne wrote a series of letters to her sister-in-law Johanna St. John, whom she addresses as Sweet Sister.

I am not able to write you a long letter. I can only say this, that tho' he lies under as much misery almost as human man can bear, yet he bears his sufferings with so much patience and resignation to God's will, that I confess I take more comfort in him under this visitation, than ever I did in all his life before.

As Rochester suffered a painful and lingering death, Anne was not unaware of the gossip that circulated at Court, claiming he was 'disordered' and that his religious conversion was the 'words of a madman.' She wrote to Johanna –

This last night if you had heard him pray, I am sure you would not have took his words for the words of a mad man, but such as come from a better spirit than the mind of mere man. But let the wicked of the world say what they please of him, the reproaches of them are an honour to him, and I take comfort, that the devil rages against my son; it shows his power over him is subdued in him, and that he has no share in him.

Rochester died on 26 July, 1680. He was 33 years old. Anne had outlived all three of her sons.

Towards the end of her life Anne continued to fight for her family's inheritance. In the winter of 1685/6, she wrote urgently to her grandson Edward Henry Lee, Earl of Lichfield. She begged, bullied and pretty much ordered him to challenge a deed supposedly made by his cousin Anne Wharton on her death bed, bequeathing her large Lee family estate to her husband Thomas. Convinced that the document had been produced under duress, and possibly fraudulently signed, Anne was anxious that her grandson should challenge the deed in collaboration with another cousin and claim what was their rightful Lee inheritance.

Anne knew all about business and legal challenges and fighting to keep hold of property. She had received plenty of practice under the most difficult of circumstances and she remained a fighter until the end of her long life.

In her 70s Anne, the woman who found Lydiard a tad boring, moved to the upwardly mobile area of Soho, London. She occupied one of two properties later owned by the Carlisle family both of which confusingly became known as Carlisle House. The house on the east side of Soho Square was demolished in 1791 and later became the site of St Patrick's Church built in 1891. Anne's home was on the west side of Soho Square and survived until 1941 when it was destroyed during a bombing raid in the Second World War.

It was here that Anne revised her will and added a codicil and as ever family came first. To the Countess of Lichfield, the wife of her grandson Edward, she bequeathed 'my best Cabinet in my Drawing Roome Table Stands and Looking glass in that Roome in London,' along with chairs and hangings 'wrought with my own work' provided she leaves them to her son Quarrendon.

Her granddaughter the Countess of Sandwich, John Wilmot's daughter Elizabeth, receives Anne's 'library of Books from the gray closet at Adderbury' and three family portraits. Lady Anne Greville, and Lady Mallet Vaughan, Wilmot's other two daughters, also receive family portraits and china and various other items. Even Anne's great granddaughters get a bequest. Lady Bridget Bertie receives items that once belonged to her mother Eleanor Lee and 'a Diamond Locket with the Duchess of Yorks hair' while Lady Charlotte Lee receives 'my gold watch and ten Jacobus peeces of old gold.' Her sister-in-law, Johanna St John receives 'my Lamp Clock which usuall Stands in my Chamber and My Turky ring set with six Diamonds.'

Anne died on 18 March, 1696 having left clear instructions for her burial in her Will.

I desire to be imbalmed but not imbowelled and to be put in Lead as the rest of my ffamily hath been and to be carried directly to Spelsbury Church wheresoever I dye and to be put into the Vault where my husbands lye and which I made after the death of Sir ffrances Henry Lee my first husband in the minority of my eldest son Sir Henry Lee.

It is too easy to describe Anne as an interfering old battle axe, curmudgeonly and controlling. During her long life she had known bereavement and loss on an unbearable scale. Her youthful love and first husband died at just 24 years old, her daughter as a child. Three brothers and two members of her extended and politically divided family had been slaughtered during the Civil Wars and she outlived a second husband and all three of her sons. She had lived through dangerous times, had risked her fortune, even her life. Maybe she wasn't a cosy granny figure but she loved her grandchildren ferociously and always acted in their best interests – although perhaps sometimes they didn't always appreciate her meddling.

Lady Johanna St John

THERE ARE FOUR stunning portraits of Lady Johanna in Lydiard House. One of her wearing an eye-catching salmon pink sash with jewels in her hair hangs in the State Drawing Room and is attributed to John Michael Wright, painted *c.*1665. The work of John Michael Wright grew in popularity during the early Restoration period when he worked alongside court favourite Peter Lely. Wright provided a quality product at a cheaper price which no doubt appealed to the frugal nature of Sir Walter and Lady Johanna.

The portrait of a very young Johanna attributed to Godfrey Kneller is slightly more perplexing. Kneller is famed for his Hampton Court Beauties, a series of portraits commissioned by Queen Mary in the 1690s. But by this date Johanna was 60 so obviously this portrait was not painted when Kneller was at the zenith of his popularity. This portrait of Johanna hangs in the State Bedroom and depicts her in a state of déshabillé. With her low-cut gown, she looks very at home here, as if she has climbed straight out of the grand four poster bed beneath. This portrait is much more in the style of Peter Lely's Windsor Beauties painted in the 1660s and which includes a portrait of Johanna's courtesan cousin Barbara Castlemaine. But would the teenage Johanna (or

Johanna St. John, wife of Sir Walter St. John, 3rd Bt.

more importantly her Puritanical father Sir Oliver St John) have ever consented to her being painted in this pose?

The two portraits of Lady Johanna and Sir Walter that hang in the library at Lydiard House are believed to have been the work of Mary Beale. A diary kept by the artist's husband records that Sir Walter began sitting for his wife on 20 September, 1677. The three-quarter length portrayal depicts Lady Johanna in middle age set against a classically inspired backdrop featuring a column and an urn. A small spaniel sits on a table to her right and places a paw on her arm. The materials and the composition are stylistically consistent with the work of Mary Beale, one of the first female artists to earn her living by her work. Johanna wears a black hooded shawl in a more sombre representation attributed to the English School of painting. This portrait of Johanna hangs in the Drawing Room at Lydiard House.

Johanna was born in the winter of 1629/30 and baptised at High Laver on 27 January, 1630. Her father, politician Oliver St. John had a somewhat varied career. In 1629 he was briefly imprisoned for circulating material with 'design of sedition'. The document was written by Sir Robert Dudley in 1614 and proposed the establishment of a military government and prerogative rule in England. This perilous situation may explain why Johanna's mother retreated to her stepfather's home at High Laver following the birth of her daughter.

Yet despite his defence of John Hampden, a Puritan landowner who refused to pay Charles I's contentious Ship Tax, the King appointed Oliver St. John Solicitor General in 1641. However, by the outbreak of the Civil War St. John had firmly aligned himself with Oliver Cromwell, and was recognised as a leading figure in the parliamentarian camp. Kinship ties with the Cromwell family had already been established; St. John's first wife Johanna was descended from Cromwell's cousin Elizabeth and after her death Oliver St. John went on to marry Elizabeth Cromwell, another of Cromwell's cousins.

In 1648 Oliver St. John was appointed Lord Chief Justice of the Common Pleas. The Lord Chancellor, Edward Hyde, Earl of Clarendon described him 'as a man reserved and of dark and clouded countenance, very proud, conversing with very few and those men of his own humour and inclinations. He was very seldom known to smile.'

Johanna appears to have grown up at various homes in Essex and London until her father acquired Thorpe Manor, Peterborough. It is probably fair to say that Johanna's upbringing during these traumatic times of political and religious conflict was a rather serious affair.

In 1649, not yet out of her teens, Johanna married Walter St. John. The couple were distantly related, Johanna descending from the senior Bletsoe branch of the St. John family and Walter from the cadet or junior Lydiard Tregoze branch. Both traced their ancestry back to Margaret Beauchamp and her first husband Sir Oliver St. John. It is likely that the weddings of both Johanna to Walter in 1649 and her sister Catherine to his brother Henry in the following year, took place in the parish church at Enfield where the sisters appear to have lived at Forty Hall, in the 1650s.

Lady Johanna and Sir Walter made their permanent home in the St. John's Battersea manor house. It was more conveniently located for Westminster where Sir Walter had a long, if undistinguished political career. The spacious manor house on the banks of the River Thames was for some time also home to Johanna's sister Catherine and her husband Henry St. John. Lady Johanna St. John and her sister-in-law, Anne Countess of Rochester were close friends, despite a fourteen-year age difference and in Johanna's letters dated 1656-1672 there are references to dining with the Countess at Ditchley. When Anne's libertine son, John Wilmot, 2nd Earl of Rochester was dying in 1680 Anne wrote several letters to Johanna who sent 'waters' to Rochester's home in Woodstock, Oxfordshire.

Living at Battersea, Lady Johanna was perfectly situated to observe the development of London. In a letter dated October 1661 written to her steward Thomas Hardyman, responsible for the smooth running of the Lydiard estate, she mentions: 'they are making a bridg from Chelsey hither over the thams.' Work must have come to a halt as the earliest bridge at Chelsea dates from 1771. These words survive in a collection of letters transcribed by Canon Brian Carne, and published in the Friends of Lydiard Tregoz Reports and provide an intimate glimpse into the life and times of Lady Johanna.

Johanna had supported the Parliamentarians during the Civil Wars but like her sister-in-law Anne, Countess of Rochester, she had to tread carefully, negotiating the Interregnum period and the Restoration. With the return of the King, Johanna was quick to invite him to dine at her Battersea home, even if her husband had been slow to affirm his allegiance. Johanna continued to do her best to redress her husband's tardiness in kissing the King's hand and when Charles expressed a desire for some Muscovy ducks to stock St James Park, Johanna wrote to Hardyman urging him to shop around. He is not, however, to let it be known who the ducks are for as Lady Johanna wants to impress the King before anyone else hears of his request.

Sir Walter and Lady Johanna made good use of the Lydiard estate for holidays and entertaining, and with the help of Hardyman, Lady Johanna kept a tight rein on Lydiard affairs. Juggling the domestic arrangements of the Wiltshire household along with her Battersea home nothing escaped her attention. Dissatisfied with the condition of the poultry shipped up to Battersea Johanna wrote to Hardyman: 'tell bes I hope to se better Turkyes and gees of her fatting for hetherto thers we have had doth not commend her huswifry.' She adds: 'I expect to here of our chees I hope you have sent them.' Johanna ordered a large amount of produce from her country estate to be delivered to Battersea where the couple regularly entertained, and Lady Johanna's housekeeping letters frequently read like a shopping list – 'a brace of deer – som butter chees and rabbits.'

The St. John country estate provided a retreat from London and city life and when disease was rampant Lady Johanna sent her children to Lydiard out of the way of contagion and also to recuperate after illness. In letters dated 1660 to Thomas Hardyman reference is made to her eight-year-old son Harry who is staying at Lydiard with his sister Johanna while another sister, ten-year-old Anne (Nan) recovers from smallpox. 'Tel (Hary) that if I here he prays and reads and gits his catikisme perfect before I come I wil bring him some fine thing Dec 1660'

In the summer of 1663, a visit was expected at Lydiard from the Lord Chancellor, Edward Hyde, a St. John family friend and kinsman, along with forty others, and was causing Lady Johanna some consternation. She wrote to Thomas Hardyman on 28 July:

I have had several cooks commended but shal not resolve on
which to take til I returne hither from Brampton a gardener
I shal then provide I might have had a very good servant who
lived with my La Brown of oxFordsher bt I think he is a papist
so I wil let him alone Sr W has bin to chuse wine to day Bid
smith se the house scowered clean all the rooms and places
and dusted downe and if you can bespeak thos who use to
git provision to git us som phesant polts and partridges and
Quails.

Lady Johanna's letters to Hardyman frequently include
instructions for the Lydiard gardener.

I have according to my promise sent Rudler downe some
seeds and some poppy Eminy roots I shal also commaund
Richard to send him a noat of the number and how to use
them but the seed must not be s[own] till next yere tel him
he must not brag to much least he lose them and tel him I
would have all the white and yelow crowns planted in the
outward garden as wel as thos that are turned plaine red or
yalow or white bid him also save some of his white stock
seed for us ...

So, what did Lady Johanna do, apart from promote her
husband's political career; entertain the King and influential
members of 17th-century society; organise the two estates at
Lydiard and Battersea and give birth to thirteen children?
     The job description for the 17th-century chatelaine included
a basic knowledge of home remedies, recipes to cool a fever
and treat an inflammation, but Johanna's expertise far exceeded
this. Lady Johanna collected recipes for pills and potions for
every conceivable complaint from the mundane to the morbid.
Johanna recorded not only her own remedies but those she had
gathered from family and friends and eminent physicians of
the day. Entries in Lady Johanna St. John's Booke 1680 include
'My Lady Beaumonts water for Palsyes Mother Appoplexes &

Convultions & Melancholy' and 'My Lady Warwicks Juyce of Liquorish' which rubs shoulders with 'Prince Ruperts oyntment for a Flux tho Blood Alsoe for Burnes & new wounds'. Lady Littleton's remedy for a 'scald head' contains 'Gunpowder beat fine put it into strong viniger stir them well let it settle skim of the cream & rub that well in'.

There are remedies for ague (a malarial type of fever sometimes resulting in convulsions) and gout, common 17th-century

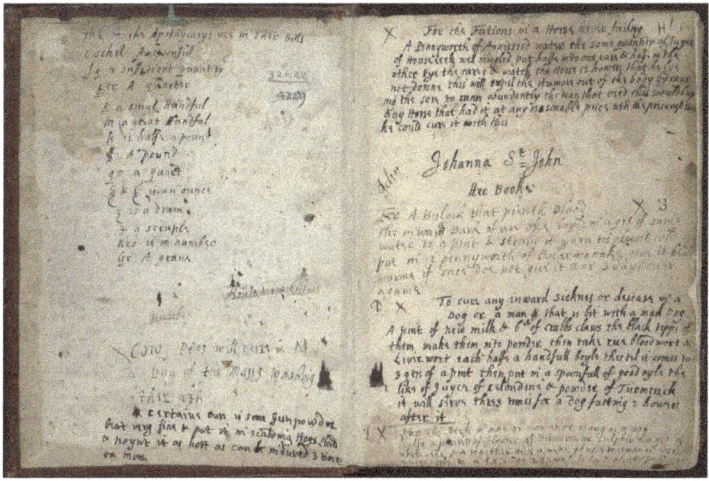

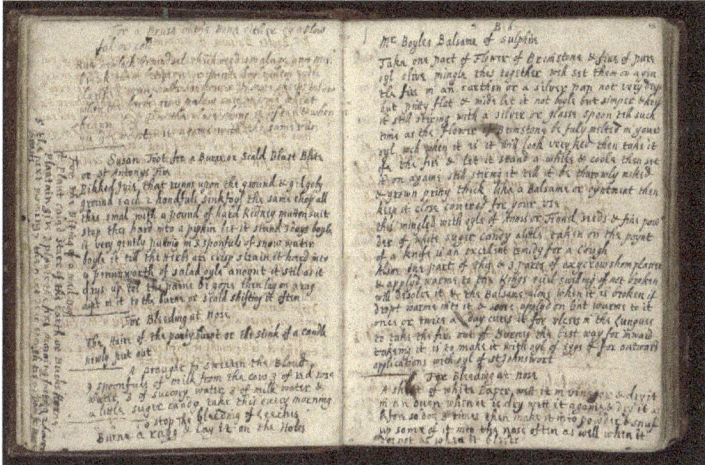

Lady Johanna St. John's 1680 book is held at the Wellcome Library and is available to view on the website.

complaints and numerous medicines for female conditions; 'For the Mother' during and after childbirth and others 'For Melancholly & madness'. One reference is 'For Melancholy the medicine wch cured my Lady Bernard' (Lady Johnna's sister Elizabeth married to Sir John Bernard 2nd Baronet.)

Lady Johanna gives special recommendation for a couple of cure-alls. She considers 'The vertues of Gilberts water' which she says is 'bad for noething' and

> cures wind & the colick restoreth decayed nature good for a consumption expels poison & all infection from the Hart helps disgestion purifies the blood gives motion to the spirits drives out the smalpox for the grippes in yong children weomen in Labor bringeth the Afterberth stops flouds for sounding & Faintings.

'The vertues of the French Balm' is equally efficacious.

> It cure new wounds in 24 hours the sore being washt in Luke warm water & wine all paines in the head anoywting the Temples it cures deafness if not natural by droping some into the eare & stoping it with cotton cures paines in the stomach & vomiting helps disgestion anointing & laying warm Flannel the wormes in children anoywting ther bellys paines & Aches any where ulcers in the Leggs or elsewhere tho never so old venomous Bittings washing the place with wine & laying on the Balm upon Lint to cause urin anointing the Belly & keines & for seatica & all cold causes.

In her will Lady Johanna left her 'great recit book' thought to be her book of medicinal recipes, to her eldest daughter Anne Cholmondeley. Lady Johanna St. John's book is now held at the Wellcome Library, a repository of books, manuscripts and archives recording the history of medicine.

On 7 March, 1703 Johanna signed the will she had written herself on three sides of foolscap folio paper, complete with numerous additions and deletions, which would result in probate being delayed. The document contains several endearing bequests, giving a glimpse of the softer side of the strict puritanical Lady Johanna. 'To my old & Deare Friend the Countess of Lindsey I leave my Gold cupp wch Mrs Drax left me for a legesey and I wish I could leave her a Friend may love her as much & have more power to serve her then my selfe.' She expressed concern for her elderly husband – 'I desire if Sir Walter St John out live me his old servants may be continued about him and that he may not be removed to Liddiard London or any other place from Battersea wher he has lived so long least it hasten his Death.'

Lady Johanna died on 15 January, 1704 aged 74 years of age. She was buried in the St. John family vault at St Mary's, Battersea a week later. In contravention of the Burying in Woollen Acts 1666-80, established to protect the home-grown industry, Lady Johanna was buried in silk for which the family had to pay a penalty fine of 50 shillings.

Barbara Villiers, Countess Castlemaine

How best to describe Barbara Villiers? Promiscuous, cunning, avaricious? She was all of these and more. Lecherous diarist Samuel Pepys had a soft spot for her though and there is an account in his diary, which shows her in a different light. On 23 August, 1662 the newly married King and Queen moved from up river Hampton Court to Whitehall, and of course Barbara with her baby son were there as well. Pepys wrote: 'there happened a scaffold below to fall, and we feared some hurt, but there was none but she [Barbara] of all the great ladies only run down among the common rabble to see what hurt was done, and did take care of a child that received some little hurt, which me thought so noble.' But then maybe he was a bit biased. He frequently referred to her as 'lovely Lady Castlemaine,' but not everyone was a member of her fan club. That other 17th-century diarist John Evelyn called her 'a strumpet' and 'an impudent woman' and famously described her as 'another Lady of Pleasure & curse of our nation.'

Some accounts say she had an abundance of auburn hair, others that she was a brunette with striking blue eyes, or perhaps they were violet, and if you thought Peter Lely's portraits of the Restoration ladies had a certain sameness about them, it was because his sitters requested that he include a likeness to the Royal favourite. A portrait of Barbara painted by Lely hangs in the State Bedroom at Lydiard House, which is a pretty appropriate setting for the lady who spent a lot of time in bedrooms of one sort or another.

Barbara has suffered a pretty bad press for more than 300 years. It's a little too easy to describe Barbara as reprehensible, for this would create a two-dimensional figure and she was never that simple or straightforward. She had a volatile temper and was heard on several occasions to threaten to kill her children in her attempts to control the King. That other Royal mistress Nell Gwyn, the original tart with a heart, has always been portraited as more loveable, but it is worth noting that she was also capable of pulling a stunt or two to get her own way. Her habit of calling her son 'you little bastard' in front of the King secured his title, Earl of Burford.

Barbara was born in 1641, the daughter of William Villiers, Viscount Grandison and his young wife Mary Bayning. William was the son of Sir Edward Villiers and his wife Barbara St. John who grew up at Lydiard House and after whom Barbara was named.

Barbara was born as Charles I locked horns with parliament and war ensued. Her father William, like his three cousins, the sons of her uncle Sir John St. John, fought for the Royalists during the English Civil Wars raising a regiment for the King's army. He fought in the Siege of Bristol in August 1643 when he was fatally wounded and died at Oxford on 30 September where he was buried in Christ Church Cathedral.

Barbara would later erect a magnificent, marble monument to her father in the cathedral. A translation of the Latin inscription reads:

Barbara Villiers, Countess Castlemaine and Duchess of Cleveland.
Granddaughter of Barbara St. John and Charles II's mistress.

Here lies buried William Villiers, Viscount Grandison
of Limerick.

In him the arts of war (Mars) and of peace (the Graces)
competed for the pre-eminence,/he increased the dignity of a
most handsome presence by his most illustrious deeds./ After
very great achievements in Belgium, Ireland, and finally in
England, he – while leading his troops from Royalist areas
to besieged Bristol against the rebels – was the first to cross
the outer defences when the scaling ladders were brought

up./ In more senses than one did he discharge the office of a leader:/ he thus inspired the valour – or even the shame – of the soldier that he might capture the defences./ Meanwhile his thigh had been pierced by a bullet, and he interwove the cypress [symbol of death] with the laurel [symbol of victory] – too great a price to be paid for the capture of the city./ He was carried back to Oxford and died towards the end of the month of August 1643 in his thirtieth year./ Moved by filial piety Barbara, Duchess of Cleveland, erected this monument to the best of parents

Edward Hyde, Earl of Clarendon would later write of William that: 'He was a young man of so virtuous a habit of mind, that no temptation or provocation could corrupt him; so great a lover of justice and integrity, that no example, necessity, or even the barbarity of this war, could make him swerve from the most precise rules of it; and of that rate piety and devotion, that the court or camp could not shew a more faultless person, or to whole example young men might more reasonably conform themselves.' So, Barbara didn't take after him then.

William's young widow Mary, barely out of her teens, had sole responsibility for her young daughter Barbara, not yet three years old. In 1648 Mary married Charles, Second Earl of Anglesea, a cousin of her late husband, who also rallied behind the Royal cause.

Some historians say that Barbara was raised in comparative poverty, her day-to-day existence one of uncertainty. Perhaps the post war years of insecurity during her early childhood were answerable for planting the seed of avarice that contributed to Barbara's notoriety. She certainly learned to live by her wits, using both her family connections but most especially her physical attributes to her best advantage. Barbara was a survivor, manipulating the men she met on her way to the most sought-after bed, that of the king in exile Charles Stuart.

Barbara doesn't appear to have had many female friends but she certainly had a lot of male admirers. Her list of lovers was long and included Philip Stanhope, Lord Chesterfield and even her kinsman John Churchill, later created Duke of Marlborough.

Like her mother, Barbara married young. Her husband Roger Palmer was a courtier and well connected and most important, he was compliant. The couple were married on 14 April, 1659 at St Gregory by St Paul in the City of London. That same year they joined the exiled Court in the Hague.

The Palmers were among those who accompanied Charles on his triumphant return to England in 1660 and it was rumoured that the King spent his first night in Whitehall Palace in the company of Barbara. Nine months later Barbara gave birth to a daughter whom Palmer claimed as his own. However little Anne was most commonly known as Anne Fitzroy, a name given to bastard royal children, and by the time of her marriage in 1674 aged just thirteen she was acknowledged as the King's daughter and created Lady Sussex.

It was a bit tricky knowing the father of any of Barbara's children, but Charles gamely accepted responsibility for five of them. He baulked at acknowledging her sixth child, a daughter named Barbara, who was generally thought to be John Churchill's daughter.

Historians are divided as to where Barbara's second child, a boy named Charles, was born. Thomas Seccombe, assistant editor of the 1885-1900 edition of the *Dictionary of National Biography* claims the child was born at the Palmer's home in King Street, Westminster. However, today it is more widely believed that Barbara spent her confinement at Hampton Court Palace where the King and his new wife were honeymooning at the time.

Barbara reigned as uncrowned Queen and she wasn't going to let the arrival of the official candidate, Portuguese princess Catherine of Braganza, cramp her style. Barbara first demanded that she be admitted as one of the Queen's Maids of Honour and then that she be publicly acknowledged as the King's 'official mistress' the *Maitresse-en-Titre*. With the birth of her son Barbara's influence over the King was at its zenith.

In 1662 she somewhat surprisingly converted to Catholicism. Many at court questioned her possible motives as she had never previously displayed any great religious conviction and by so doing, she was compelled to resign her hard-won post as Lady of the Bedchamber to the Queen.

Then in 1663 Frances Stewart arrived on the scene fresh from Paris to be maid of honour to the Queen. Charles was soon besotted. Barbara was not happy. But she still had a few tricks up her sleeve.

On 5 September, 1664 Barbara gave birth to her fourth child, a daughter born at Whitehall Palace, but the news was not made public. These were critical times; the populace was frustrated with their ineffective monarch and resentful of the influence Barbara had upon him. A document in the Domestic State Papers dated 1666 declared 'people say, 'Give the King the Countess of Castlemaine, and he cares not what the nation suffers.'

Thomas Povey, a London merchant, politician and member of the Council for Foreign Plantations said: 'the King hath taken ten times more care and pains in making friends between my Lady Castlemaine and Mrs Stewart, when they have fallen out, than ever he did to save his kingdom.' Philip Walsingham Sergeant wrote in *My Lady Castlemaine* published in 1912 that: 'In spite of his [the King] belief that women did not rule him, Lady Castlemaine's hand was in all his affairs, political and financial.'

Just weeks after giving birth Barbara was set upon in St James's Park, returning from an evening spent at the Palace with the Duchess of York. Her assailants sought merely to frighten her, reminding her of the fate of another King's mistress, Jane Shore, abandoned by Edward IV.

Undaunted, Barbara continued to accept bribes from the Spanish and the French and appeared to have direct access to the Privy Purse account from which she made withdrawals at will. In 1666, along with all the expensive gifts, Charles paid around £30,000 to clear her debts.

As the babies arrived in quick succession so did titles and property, and money. In 1668-9 Barbara received an annual grant of £4,700 out of the revenue of the Post Office. Charles had intended this as an inducement to persuade her to retire to France. Barbara, being Barbara, took the money, and stayed put.

John Evelyn mentioned in his diary seeing Barbara at a theatre production of the *Trajedie of Horace* in 1668 when he described her as 'esteemed at 40000 pounds & more: & far out shining the Queene etc:'

In 1670 Louise de Keroualle arrived from France as maid of honour to Charles's sister Henrietta Anne, Duchess of Orleans. By 1671 she was the King's mistress and in 1673 gave birth to a son Charles, later 1st Duke of Richmond and Lennox. Barbara was created Duchess of Cleveland and Baroness Nonsuch as a consolation prize, inheriting the sumptuous Nonsuch Palace built by Henry VIII in 1538. But the corrupt countess found the property a drain on her finances, so after she had stripped it and sold everything of value, she applied for permission to knock it down and then sold the fabric of the building, all to offset her gambling debts.

The rise in favour of new Royal mistress, Louise de Keroualle, saw Barbara also widen her romantic scope. There were frequent affairs including liaisons with playwright William Wycherley and acrobat Jacob Hall. But by now Barbara's days as Royal favourite were numbered. Her constant demands and bad behaviour saw the King grow weary of her as he cast his net for a more amenable and younger bedfellow. With the arrival on the scene of Nell Gwyn, Barbara was asked to vacate her apartments in Whitehall.

In 1676 Barbara at last moved to Paris, an event that had been long anticipated, not least by the King. As a parting gift Charles made a new grant to her of the offices of Chief Steward of Hampton Court and Keeper of the Chace. She left behind in England her youngest daughter Barbara to the care of the Sisters of the Convent of the Immaculate Conception of Our Blessed Lady. At twelve years of age daughter Charlotte was already married. Her wayward eldest daughter Anne, Countess of Sussex she took with her and placed her in a religious house at Conflans.

And then Barbara set about having herself a good time. After all, Charles had moved on.

She reminded him in a letter written from Paris in 1678 that he had bid her: 'Madam, all that I ask of you for your own sake is, live so for the future as to make the least noise you can, and I care not who you love.' She only returned to England occasionally, usually when her children were being recognised by their father. In 1682 she came home to see her son the Duke of Grafton presented by the King with a commission as Colonel of the Foot Guards. But the anti-Catholic fervour grew frighteningly close and even as a former Royal Mistress she was not above suspicion when it came to the King's safety.

Charles died in 1685, his children and mistresses left well provided for, his Kingdom rather less so. In his diary Evelyn records at length the circumstance of the death of Charles II, who he described as 'an excellent prince doubtlesse had he ben lesse addicted to Women.' He recorded the King's last instructions to his brother James, Duke of York that he 'be kind to his Concubines the DD: of Cleveland & especially Portsmouth, & that Nelly might not starve.'

Did Barbara ever have a true affection for the King or was she only interested in the perks that came with the job? There was no stopping the indomitable duchess who had an affair with actor Cardonell Goodman after the king's death, when she was in her mid-forties, and supposedly gave birth to another son.

In 1700 Barbara moved into a property on Chiswick Mall, known today as Walpole House after the 18th-century politician Thomas Walpole who later lived there. In 1705 her long estranged husband, Roger Palmer, died and just four months later Barbara made a disastrous second marriage to Major General Robert 'Beau' Fielding. Unfortunately, General Fielding had married heiress Anne Deleau just days before marrying Barbara. However, it turned out he too had been duped and had married not the wealthy lady but a mere servant girl in disguise. Barbara eventually prosecuted him for bigamy.

Barbara lived out her later years at Chiswick where she cared for her grandson Charles Hamilton, the illegitimate son of her daughter Barbara and even as late as 1708, a year before her death, she was still on the Royal pension roll, receiving £100 a week. She died on Sunday 9 October, 1709 from the effects of dropsy, a condition that had seen her swell to a great size and destroyed her famous beauty. She was buried four days later in the churchyard at St Nicholas, Chiswick, her coffin carried by four peers and two dukes. A spectral Lady Castlemaine is said to revisit her Chiswick home on stormy nights, when she acts threateningly if approached. Sounds like Barbara.

The Lely portrait was sold by Vernon, 6th Viscount Bolingbroke when he wound up the estate in the 1940s. It eventually returned to Lydiard House in 1982 following fund raising by Thamesdown Borough Council with financial support from the Victoria and Albert Museum and the National Heritage Memorial Fund.

5

Love and Marriage

Mary Rich

M ARY RICH WAS not one of the big players on the St. John stage. She left no known imprint on the Lydiard estate and no written record. If Mary supervised planting in Lady Johanna's garden, we don't know of it. If she was a dutiful daughter in law or a sisterly confidante, we don't know of that either. There are two known portraits of Lady Mary Rich, one painted by Sir Peter Lely and another by Henry Gascar seated with her sister Lady Anne Barrington, but sadly neither of them hangs in Lydiard House. Mary's sole legacy is that she was the mother of Henry St. John, 1st Viscount Bolingbroke, Secretary at War to Queen Anne, friend of Swift and Pope, who ducked and dived throughout a tumultuous political career.

The 17th-century English Civil Wars had divided families, set neighbour against neighbour and friend against friend. Throughout this tumultuous period the St. John family suffered similarly, and it was most frequently the women who straddled the difficult political divide with diplomacy, skill and in some cases, cunning. Lady Johanna St. John, daughter of the Cromwellian supporter Sir Oliver St. John, Chief Justice of the Common Pleas, learned how to play the perfect post-Restoration hostess to Charles II, and when she sought a suitable son for her wayward son, she chose a family who had also hedged their bets.

Lady Mary Rich was the granddaughter of staunch Puritan, Robert Rich, 2nd Earl of Warwick, who had begun the war on one side but eventually changed his political alliance. In 1642 Robert was appointed Lord Lieutenant of Essex and Lord High

Admiral and secured the Navy for the Parliamentarians at the outbreak of war. Mary's father, the 3rd Earl of Warwick, was a Royalist, so perhaps Lady Johanna was covering all bases.

Mary was the second of three daughters born to Robert, 3rd Earl of Warwick and his wife Anne. Following the death of their parents in 1659 Mary and her two sisters were placed in the care of Charles Rich, their father's younger brother who succeeded to the title. It is likely that Sir Walter and Johanna chose young Lady Mary Rich due to the influence of her devout aunt, Mary, Countess of Warwick. Charles and Mary had no surviving children of their own and Mary raised the girls 'as a mother' at the family home of Lees Priory, Felstead in Essex.

In her diary Mary records negotiating the marriages of her three nieces.

> About four months after my lord's death, [Charles] my Lady Mary Rich, my lord's nieces, who I had constantly bred from the time of her father's death, was married at Lees Chapel by Dr. Walker, the 11th December 1673. The match was agreed on before my lord's death, but finished by me, much to my satisfaction, because it was a very orderly and religious family, and there was a very good estate, and the young gentleman she married, Mr Henry St. John, was very good-natured and viceless, and his good father and mother, Sir Walter St. John and my Lady St. John, were very eminent for owning and practising religion. And here, O my good God, let me return thee my praises for hearing the reiterated prayers I put up to the Divine Majesty, for her being marriage settled in a family where thy sacred name was had in veneration.

There is evidence that this St. John marriage was a happy one, equal in affection given and received. The parish registers for St Andrew, Holborn record the following baptismal entry: 'Mary St John Dau: of Henry St John Esq & ye Honble ye Lady Mary St John his Wife borne in Warwick House in High Holborn bapt ye 14 February 1674 St Andrew, Holborn.' Two sons, both named

Walter, were born and died and all three infants were buried at St Mary's, Battersea.

In 1678 Mary was pregnant yet again. This time she retired to the Lydiard estate for her confinement and on 16 September was delivered of a healthy boy. Sadly, Mary died shortly after the birth and was buried at the neighbouring parish church of St Mary's, Lydiard Tregoze on 2 October. She was 26 years old. Her son was christened eight days later on 10 October at the church in Battersea.

Following the death of his young wife, Henry kicked up his heels and reappeared on the drinking and gambling scene, with dire consequences where it very nearly all went horribly wrong. A drunken argument and a proposed wager on the horses saw Henry and his cousin Edmund Richmond Webb involved in the murder of Sir William Estcourt at the Globe Tavern in 1684. Henry and Edmund were incarcerated in Newgate prison, jointly charged with murder and manslaughter and sentenced to death.

It was fortunate for Henry that his parents had some influence at court and that his cousin Barbara, Countess of Castlemaine, was a former mistress of Charles II. Henry's mother Lady Johanna raised a sum of money estimated to be £16,000 to secure a reprieve for her son while Barbara persuaded the King to remove the sentence of death and restore Henry's forfeited estate to him. Henry wisely went abroad to let the dust settle, leaving his six-year-old son at Battersea with his parents Sir Walter and Lady Johanna. But he didn't stay away long. By 26 March, 1685 he was back in England where he was returned as MP for Wootton Bassett.

Angelica Magdalena St. John

IT REMAINS UNKNOWN how much of Henry's murky past the recently widowed Angelica Wharton knew before she married him, becoming his second wife and stepmother to his young son, also named Henry.

Angelica was born in around 1664, one of George Pelissary and his wife Madeleine Bibaud's four children. Originating in Italy, the spelling of the Pellisary name changed as the family moved about Europe. In the 16th century they moved to Switzerland and

Angelica Magdalena Pelissary, second wife of Henry, 1st Viscount St. John.

settled in Geneva where they joined the strict, Calvinist Protestant church. Angelica's grandparents would eventually move across the border to France where her father George was born in around 1630 and received French nationality in 1647.

George became adviser to Louis XIV, first director general of the French West India Company and Treasurer General of Marines and Superintendent of Ship and Galleys to the King. Angelica grew up in a religious and cultured household. Among the guests invited to her parents' home were poets, academics and members of the French nobility.

But in October 1685 Louis XIV revoked the Edict of Nantes and those practising the reformed Protestant faith either converted to Catholicism or went in fear of their lives. Young Angelica was among the 200,000 French Protestants who fled the country for one where they could practise their religion safely. She arrived in London sometime in 1684 and married Philip Wharton, the recently appointed Warden of the London Mint. Their marriage was sadly a brief affair as Philip died in February 1684/5, but he left Angelica well provided for with £6,000 worth of East India Company stock.

Less than a year after Wharton's death Angelica met Sir Henry St. John. Angelica could hardly have escaped hearing news of the murder that was the talk of the town, but the couple soon married. The wedding took place at St Anne's Church, Soho on 1 January, 1686/7. Following their marriage, the newlyweds set up home in Bury Street Westminster, later moving to Berkeley Street and then Albermarle Street, Piccadilly. Visits to their country estate at Lydiard Park were frequent and lengthy, sometimes extending from early June through to November. Where like many other St. John ladies, Angelica took an interest in the Lydiard gardens and the fashionable fruits of the day. Her daughter Henrietta Knight, Lady Luxborough mentioned in one of her letters:

> The late King George [I] was fond of peaches stewed in
> brandy in a particular manner, which he had tasted at my
> father's, and ever after until his death, my mamma furnished

him with a sufficient quantity to last the year round (he eating two every night); this little present he took kindly but one season proved fatal to fruit trees, and she could present His Majesty but with half the usual quantity, desiring him to use economy, for they would scarce serve him the year at one each night. Being thus forced by necessity to retrench, he said he would then eat two every other night; and valued himself upon having mortified himself less than if he had yielded to their regulation of one each night, which I suppose may be called a compromise between economy and epicurism.

The first of Henry and Angelica's children, a boy named Walter after his St. John grandfather, was born on 13 June, 1688 and christened two weeks later at St Anne's Soho, the church where his parents had married. Sadly, little Walter did not live to celebrate his first birthday and was buried on 4 May, 1689 in the St. John family vault at St Mary's, Battersea.

Angelica went on to have a further eleven children; all but four of them died in infancy – Oliver, Anne, Pawlet, Charlotte, Isabella, Johanna and a second son named Walter. George, born in 1693 died in Venice in 1716 age 23. John, 2nd Viscount St. John born in 1702 died in Naples in 1748 age 46; Holles was born in 1710 and died in 1738 age 28 and Henrietta born in 1699 died in 1756 age 56 years.

In 1736 Angelica's family was wreaked by scandal yet again when her daughter Henrietta, married to Robert Knight, Lord Luxborough, had an inappropriate relationship. The scandal and Henrietta's humiliation were made very public. Angelica rushed to her daughter's side, advising her to plead for forgiveness, but Knight was not a forgiving man.

With her constitution worn down by so many pregnancies, it was thought this final blow hastened Angelica's end. She died on 5 August, 1736.

'Dear Lady St Jean is dead, I think it is the best thing she has done since she came into the world,' wrote Marie Claire, the second wife of Henry, Viscount Bolingbroke, to her friend the

Countess of Denbigh in a letter dated 25 October, 1736. 'They say her husband and children are no more grieved about it than I am.'

Of what devilish dealings and grave crimes had the recently departed Angelica Magdalena St. John been found guilty? Described as shy, lacking confidence and speaking very little English, Angelica had done nothing to receive such a vitriolic, posthumous attack.

Henry, Viscount Bolingbroke, the young stepson she had loved and cared for, wrote to Robert Knight, his brother-in-law, that he felt 'neither joy nor sorrow' at the death of his stepmother. 'Silly as she was, she had not enough to be ye cause, during a long course of years of much mischief. A wise woman would have found her account better in a contrary conduct.' And to his half-brothers Jack and Holles he wrote: 'I cannot be hypocrite enough to condole.'

But at least the profligate husband she had supported during 50 years of marriage appreciated her worth, telling the same Robert Knight when she was dying that he would 'lose a virtuous and good wife and you a good relation and friend.'

Sadly, even Angelica's funeral was tarnished by the ridiculous, recalled in *The Merry Wives of Battersea and Gossip of Three Centuries* written by A.M. Wilhelmina Stirling from an account which had appeared in the *London Daily Post and General Advertiser* on Friday, 13 August, 1736.

> For some unexplained reason her corpse was enclosed in three coffins and the weight was such that the bearers, unable to support it, let it fall to the ground, when one of them [Robert Ball] endeavouring to save it, had his arm broken. It was afterwards taken up, we are told, and decently conveyed to the church door, but the entrance was found to be so low as not to admit it to be carried on the men's shoulders, so that they were obliged to convey it on rollers from thence to a place of interment.

There are three portraits of Angelica at Lydiard House. Probably the most resplendent of these is the one that hangs in the State Bedroom. This full-length portrait painted by the circle of John Vanderbank shows a mature Angelica dressed in her Coronation robes and holding her coronet.

A smaller, oval portrait of a much younger Angelica hangs in the State Drawing Room. Her long, brown hair curls over her shoulder and her dark eyes look into those of the beholder. This portrait is painted in the style of Godfrey Kneller. A third portrait, which also hangs in the State Drawing Room, was once unidentified but is now thought to be that of a young Angelica, painted by Enoch Seeman the younger.

As for Henry, well he lived on and on and it appeared that the whole family couldn't wait for him to die. Marie Claire de Marcilly, the wife of his eldest son Henry, wrote to her friend the Countess of Denbigh calling him '*le pere eternal*' the undying father, 'he just keeps himself alive and that is all. God will take him when it pleases Him nobody on this earth will regret him, and Heaven with not gain much by it.' Another daughter in law Anne Furnese commented: 'We at present propose being in Town about the 9th of December, when I don't doubt we shall be regaled with the sight of 85 more blooming than 84.' The father they called Old Frump eventually died on 8 April, 1742 aged 89.

Frances Winchcombe

T HERE CAN BE no denying that Henry St. John, 1st Viscount Bolingbroke was a brilliant and extraordinary politician, historian, philosopher and satirical journalist. But what was he like as a husband? It depends upon which of his two wives you were.

Henry was born on 16 September, 1678 at Lydiard House. Following the death of his mother, the baby was swiftly removed to his grandparents' home at Battersea, his father considered a poor candidate for unsupervised single parenthood. There he spent his childhood under the watchful eye of Sir Walter and Lady Johanna St. John.

Frances Winchcombe, first wife of Henry, 1st Viscount Bolingbroke.

He was educated first at home at Battersea before attending Eton. But despite Sir Walter and Lady Johanna's best efforts, he soon followed in the dissolute footsteps of his decadent father. By 1698 his beleaguered grandparents had despatched him on the traditional Grand Tour. Having partied his way around Europe Sir Walter and Lady Johanna, fearing for his reputation, his health and his life in the hereafter, arranged a marriage for him with Berkshire heiress Frances Winchcombe. Sir Walter also resigned his parliamentary seat at Wootton Bassett in favour of his wayward grandson, perhaps to give him some focus in life and thus began Henry's illustrious political career. He served as MP for Wootton Bassett from 1700/1 to 1708 and for Berkshire from 1710-1712. Appointed Queen Anne's Secretary at War in 1704 Henry went on to serve as Secretary of State for the Northern Department in 1710 transferring to the Southern Division in 1713.

During these exhilarating times Henry was supported by his wife Frances, the eldest daughter and co-heiress of Sir Henry Winchcombe. Henry and Frances were married on 22 May, 1701 at St Dunstan's in the East. Frances was 22 years of age and Henry a year older. The marriage register reveals the young couple were both of the parish of St James's, Westminster and that they were married by licence. Following the ceremony, the newlyweds drove through London to Chelsea where they were rowed across the river to start their married life at the St. John Battersea home still under the watchful eye of Lady Johanna.

In 1702 the young married couple moved into number 21 Golden Square, Westminster, one of two properties owned by Frances' grandmother, Lady Frances Winchcombe. They divided their time between London and the Winchcombe country estate at Bucklebury, where it is said Henry was at his most peaceful. It was here that he entertained his friends among the literati and Jonathan Swift described a visit writing: 'Mr Secretary was a perfect country gentleman at Bucklebury; he smoked tobacco with one or two neighbours; he enquired after the wheat in such a field; he went to visit his hounds, and knew all their names; he and his lady saw me to my chamber just in the country fashion.'

But what about Frances?

It is doubtful Henry gave up his debauched ways upon marriage and a letter to his partner in crime, Thomas Coke, reveal that in 1705 he was still up to his old tricks. Dated 28 May Henry wrote to Thomas who was taking the waters at Bath following the spring election. 'I am glad your election is over, your fever gone and your worship is again upon the hunt: for what the devil can carry you to Bath at this time but a whore? ... Really Tom, you are missed: whoring flags without you ...'

Totally in awe of her famous husband, Frances would appear to have little knowledge of his licentious lifestyle, at least not at the beginning of their relationship. She remained forever on the periphery of his life, appearing only briefly when he entertained at Golden Square. She seldom moved in fashionable society and did not appear to have any very intimate female friends. Perhaps it was this solitary existence that protected her from the society gossips.

In 1714, with Queen Anne desperately ill and fading fast, Henry rapidly allied himself with the Jacobites and the Queen's Catholic half-brother James, the 'Old Pretender.' Henry plotted with James while taking the oath of allegiance to the Hanoverian successor. However, the new King George hammered home the final nail in Henry's political coffin, informing him that his services were no longer required. Henry walked to the Cockpit accompanied by the Duke of Shrewsbury and Lord Cowper to watch the sealing of his papers.

Served with a Bill of Attainder, Henry was accused of privately negotiating a dishonourable and destructive peace with France while a Secretary of State for Queen Anne and of advising the surrender of Tournai to the French and Spain and the West Indies to Philip of Spain. He was considered by many as a traitor twice over and was deprived of his title, his estates and his wealth. It was, quite obviously, all over. On 27 March, 1715 Henry set sail for exile in France.

Tormented by fear for Henry following the Pretender's arrival in Scotland and with further arrests made during the Autumn of 1715, Frances took ill. 'I have been so ill that nobody expected my life,' she wrote to Henry's half-brother Jack St. John. 'I have been horribly frightened with the reports of drowning & I know not what, I am joy'd 'tis false,' she continued having just received news that Henry was safe.

Before his escape, Henry returned the property Frances had conveyed to him earlier in their marriage with instructions that she must hand it over to Sir William Wyndham and Lord Stawell to prevent its seizure by the Crown. Preserved in the British

Museum is a list of items Frances sold in order to send money to the husband she believed to be destitute. The list is titled 'An Account of Several Things Left by Lord Bolingbroke in his Lady's Hands When He Went Abroad in March 1714-5.'

Other than a diamond ring, a present to Henry from the King of France, all the items of jewellery on the list belonged to Frances, given to her by her mother and grandmother. Henry had, in fact, managed to secure £13,000 which he took with him the night he fled, so he was hardly penniless.

Frances stayed with the St. John family at Battersea while she petitioned the King to look sympathetically upon her plight. Eventually a clause signed by the King allowed Frances some access to the estate that had originally been hers. At last able to keep the house at Bucklebury in better order, Frances continued to plan for Henry's return, until gossip from France eventually broke her spirit. Henry had taken the Marquise de Villette as his mistress and was living openly with her in her chateau at Marcilly. This was the final blow that broke poor Frances' heart. Following increasingly long bouts of ill health, she eventually stopped eating.

Her doctor saw her on 24 September when he wrote: 'She just tasted a little for two or three days of some odd salt meats, but her stomach flagged again, and now it will only bear asses milk. She keeps her bed altogether and I do not think that she can last three weeks longer.' Frances died at 8 am on the morning of Friday 24 October, 1718 aged 39. She left what remained of her fortune to her nephew, Winchcombe Packer, her sister Mary's son.

On hearing this news Henry wrote in a letter to his former mistress Madam de Ferriol, 'she [Frances] has no right to dispose of Anything, in virtue of the deed of gift that I made, and the withdrawal of the forfeiture on the personal estate which the King has given her on my behalf. My bad fortune seldom flags ...' He never once expressed any regret or sadness at the death of his devoted wife.

An often repeated ghost story was associated with the sad story of Frances Winchcombe. Before the 1980s housing development was built on the edge of Lydiard Park an ethereal coach and horses was occasionally heard, driven furiously past the former Rectory. Seated inside was the distraught Frances hoping to find her errant husband holed up at Lydiard House. There has been no recent siting of the ghostly coach and four with the Rectory long gone and houses built in the fields.

There are two portraits of Frances Winchcombe in the Drawing Room at Lydiard House. With finely modelled features in an oval face and a rather serious expression, Frances was described as one of the great beauties of her day.

Marie Claire de Marcilly

WHILE FRANCES WINCHCOMBE fared badly as Henry Bolingbroke's first wife, his second, Marie Claire de Marcilly, appeared to be the love of his life.

Marie Claire des Champs was born in the chateau of Marcilly, near Nogent sur Seine in 1675, the daughter of Armand des Champs, Seigneur de Marcilly, and his wife Elizabeth Indrot. As a young woman Marie Claire made quite an impression at the glittering court of the Sun King, Louis XIV. She was described as intelligent but unassuming, vivacious, amiable and of a sweet disposition and she attracted the attention of the wealthy Chevalier de Villette. However, it was his father Philip le Valois Villett whom Marie Claire would eventually marry.

Widowed in 1707 Marie Claire inherited property and an income from her husband to add to her Marcilly wealth and appeared to be in no hurry to remarry.

The attainted Henry rented a small house in Ablon where he licked his wounds and wrote 'Reflections Upon Exile.' In 1717 Henry moved in with Marie Claire at Marcilly. The couple were said to spend their mornings taking walks about the estate and in the afternoon, they would read and talk together. Perhaps Henry had found a match for his intellect in Marie Claire that was missing in poor Frances.

Henry appeared to be a reformed character, living a life of domestic bliss, but he had lost none of his ambition and he hadn't really changed that much. While he might have appeared content in his rural retreat, Henry had not given up on his dream of returning to England and political prominence. In 1718 he left Marie Claire and moved to Paris to kick over the traces and indulge in the excesses of his former lifestyle. But it was to Marie Claire he returned when it all took a toll on his health.

Henry and Marie Claire were still unable to marry following the death of Frances. Marie Claire had invested heavily in English funds which would be seized by the Crown should she marry the outlawed Henry Bolingbroke, and neither of them could afford for this to happen.

As Frances had financially supported Henry for many years, so did Marie Claire and as Frances had petitioned for his pardon, so Marie Claire used her influential friends such as the Duchess of Kendal and Mrs Howard, mistress of the Prince of Wales, to plead his case.

Henry still had some friends in parliament who argued for him and in 1723 a pardon passed the Great Seal and he was allowed to return to England. By 1725 Henry's property had been restored and the couple settled in England and a home at Dawley near Uxbridge. However, Henry was still unable to resume his political career.

While Marie Claire and his friends tried to persuade Henry to give up on politics and concentrate on his philosophical work, others thought the situation ripe for his return and even tipped him as a contender for Prime Minister. By 1730 he was leader of the Opposition despite having no seat in either House.

Marie Claire was attributed with healing the rift between Henry and certain members of his family, including his much younger half-sister Henrietta, and was described as being extremely popular with the Battersea household. Seemingly the only blot on her character came with her cruel comment on the death of her husband's stepmother, Angelica de Pelissary.

Throughout her life Marie Claire was plagued by an unspecified internal complaint, which at times reduced her to the state of an invalid. Always less than happy living in England, she returned to

Marie Claire de Marcilly, second wife of Henry, 1st Viscount Bolingbroke.

France where Henry joined her in 1734. But if she hoped for a peaceful retirement in her homeland, she was to be disappointed. By 1744 they were back in England, living a life of near solitude at the St. John manor house in Battersea. Any political influence Henry may have clawed back, eventually extinguished.

Frustrated and in ill health, Henry was described as 'pendantick, fretful, angry with his wife' by William Pitt, an occasional visitor to Battersea. A difficult companion for the increasingly isolated Marie Claire who appears to have never acquired a proper grasp of the English language.

In a letter dated 1747 Marie Claire writes from Bath where they had gone to take the waters:

> I am lodging here in Pierre Point Street, between two parades, but with no air from either one of them – only the din of both streets during the day, and every night all the turnspit dogs of the city meet together and bark without ceasing... They say the town is very full. I see no one, nor am I likely to see anyone, especially any ladies. I am too old to make new acquaintances. I do not wear panniers nor do I speak the language.

The irascible Henry who had behaved so callously towards his first wife, the neglected Frances Winchcombe, showed nothing but love and devotion for his second, never more so than in her final months.

On December 19, 1749 Marie Claire wrote to Lady Denbigh from their house in Soho. 'My hermit and I go to bed before six o'clock. He gives himself up entirely to looking after me, in fact, this is his only occupation. It is enough to give him the spleen, but he shows no sign of it. I cannot tell you how touched I am by his love and care.'

Marie Claire died on 18 March, 1750, aged 74. 'My heart is broken, my spirit crushed and my body crippled,' Henry wrote. 'I am the most miserable of all men.' Marie Claire was buried in the parish church of St Mary's, Battersea. The inscription on her memorial composed by her grieving husband.

> Born of a noble family, bred in the Court of Lewis 14th She reflected a lustre on the former by the superior accomplishments of her mind; She was an ornament to the latter by the aimable dignity and grave of her behaviour. She lived, the honor of her own sex, the delight and admiration of ours. She dyed, an object of imitation to both, with all the firmness that religion can inspire.

Following her death, the Marechal de Montmorin, husband of Marie Claire's stepdaughter, challenged her will on the grounds that her marriage to Henry in May 1720 in Aix la Chapelle had never been legally solemnised. Without documentary evidence the French courts decided in favour of de Montmorin. Henry appealed against the judgement but by then was terminally ill. He died on 12 December, 1751, unaware that the French Chamber had reversed the decision of the courts and validated his marriage.

There is just one portrait of Marie Claire in Lydiard House, but even this is the subject of some controversy. Fashion designer and dress historian, the late Stella Mary Newton, wrote an article for the Friends of Lydiard Tregoz annual report in 1988 in which she made the following observations. 'She [Marie Claire] died in 1750, he [Henry] in 1751. But this was not the way that ladies dressed in the early years of the 18th century, nor is it the way that drapery painters represented them as being dressed. Nor were they, at that time, placed in the canvas in this manner, in a vacuum, as it were.' Ms Newton went on to suggest that the portrait was begun, but that Marie Claire died before it was completed, and that it remained unfinished until the end of the century, creating an 'appealing but extraordinary effect.'

Today the two Viscountess' Bolingbroke look down upon visitors from the walls of the State Drawing Room at Lydiard House, the enigmatic Marie Claire de Marcilly and the long-suffering Frances Winchcombe.

6

Who would live in a house like this?

Henrietta Knight, Lady Luxborough

FOR MANY OF the St. John ladies of Lydiard gardening provided a comfort in their sadness. Diana, artist wife of Frederick 'Bully' Bolingbroke sought solace in the Walled Garden, while for Henrietta Knight, her love of gardening would sustain her through exile and isolation.

Henrietta was born on 15 July, 1699 most probably at Berkeley Street, in the midst of the squabbling St. John family. Her father Henry, who had been involved in the murder of Sir William Estcourt in a pub brawl, had proved a huge disappointment to his Puritan parents Sir Walter and Lady Johanna St. John. Henrietta's half-brother, the mercurial statesman Henry St. John, Queen Anne's Secretary at War, despised his father and rebelled against the grandparents into whose protection he had been placed when Henry senior had been forced to flee the country. In the middle of this quarrelsome household Henrietta and her much older half-brother Henry formed the closest of bonds.

Henrietta spent her childhood summers in the old-fashioned, formal gardens at Lydiard Park. It was another brother John (Jack) 2nd Viscount St John, who would remodel the old house, creating the Palladian mansion that stands today.

There are three portraits of Henrietta in Lydiard House; one as a chubby cheeked two-year-old hangs in the State Drawing Room above a three-quarter length portrait attributed to the artist Maria Verelst. The third portrait of Henrietta dressed in a sumptuous gold dress hangs in the State Dining Room. Henrietta, with her mass of unfashionable black hair and tall frame, was beautiful in an unconventional way. By some she was considered intelligent and gregarious, by others frivolous and foolish with a romantic inclination, which unfortunately proved to be her downfall.

It was her brother Henry who introduced her to banker Robert Knight, the son of the Chief Cashier of the South Sea Company, a 'get rich quick' venture intended to reduce the national debt while opening spurious trading opportunities in South America and the islands in the South Sea. The company crashed in 1720, ruining thousands of investors in what became known as the South Sea Bubble. The disgraced Chief Cashier grabbed what he could and fled to France where he acquired La Planchette, a country residence near Paris.

Following a short engagement, Henrietta and Robert married by special licence at St Mary's, Battersea on 20 June, 1727. The couple set up home in Paris with Henrietta's in-laws where they lived for little over a year. Their son Harry was born in England at Henry Bolingbroke's Dawley home and a daughter named Madalena Henrietta was born in 1729 at the Knight family home in London. In May 1730 Henrietta was called upon to return to Paris to resume her role as hostess for her in-law's establishment, a separation from her two young children which would last for more than two years. During her absence the children lived with her childhood friend Frances, Lady Hertford and when not required to be in attendance upon her in-laws, Henrietta would return to England, where she stayed with the Hertfords. It was on one such visit to the Hertford family home in Marlborough during the winter of 1735/1736, that Henrietta met the handsome young poet John Dalton, tutor to the young Viscount Beauchamp.

There was never any firm proof as to the nature of Henrietta's relationship with Dalton, ten years her junior. All that emerged were some poems and an incriminating letter to Dalton found by her husband, which Henrietta claimed to be a copy or translation of another.

As soon as you were gone I employ'd myself (as it must ever be in something that suggests you) in reading over your letters,

Henrietta St. John, Lady Luxborough, daughter of Henry, 1st Viscount St. John and the first wife of Robert Knight, Baron Luxborough, Viscount Barrells and Earl of Catherlough.

which I have resolved to burn, but could not bring my heart or hand to execute what my reason told me was proper for I found after having made a large bonfire, that all remained which spoke of your passion, & none were consumed but those which necessity had made cool and indifferent, these innocent victims are sacrificed whilst the guilty ones remain as cherished proofs of what were better to forget at least if not punished. But what do I say? They are perhaps already forgot

by you or repented of How different is your stile already even
when security permits you to speak the dictates of your heart'.
pardon this reproach – perhaps my fears belie you, but I can't
help remembering the time when one hour or two brought
me some publick or private letter of your passionate tender
sentiments wrote in your own hand, in one of the latter I find
these words which I will repeat & answer 'I love you still nay
more, & must ever do so unless you pour into my wounded
soul the dear balm of your Compassion & teach me by gentle
means to conquer it.' Pardon the present answer those words
suggest to me. I have poured that balm & it has worked its
effect for your passion is conquered. I expect at least thanks
for the cure & might in vain ask the same Remedy in return
for my self for alas tis not in your power to give since Vertue
has not prevailed. Time alone can work the Cure

In her defence, Henrietta would later write to her husband:

I have read this over which in my first surprise I did not do,
& I am now sure more than ever, that I never wrote it as the
dictates of my own heart, & little thinking that I should be
thus accused, I was so impudent as to translate & coppy out a
large Bundle of such foolish letters of which I burn'd last week
to make room for things I was placing, & before God I sear
not one was other than coppys & translations, I yet flatter
myself I shall find the original of this which I would have kept
had I know it could ever be of consequence. I again repeat
that the most I ever granted to the person I am suspected of
was Compassion, which I have often accused my self of as a
crime, tho' I'm now accused of worse.

Henrietta insisted the whole business had been but a light
hearted, flirtation, her 'Platonick passion,' but Knight was having
none of it. It would appear that Henrietta's dalliance with Dalton
had not been her first transgression. A rumour had previously
circulated that Knight had discovered his wife in bed with her

physician, Dr. Peter. Perhaps the indiscretion with Dalton proved to be the final straw. There was even talk that Henrietta had given birth to another daughter in 1736 and if she had the child certainly wasn't Knights. However, the child, if there was one, was never mentioned again.

Henrietta's fate was ultimately decided upon by her husband in discussion with male members of both sides of the family. Her half-brother Henry was obviously saddened by the turn of affairs, but her other two brothers John and Holles showed little empathy for her situation. Robert Knight, hardly Mr Squeaky Clean himself, was indignant and issued his errant wife with two alternatives. She could either live in his house, confined to one floor, banned from seeing her children and deprived of pen, ink and paper to prevent her keeping in touch with her friends. Or she could retire to the Knight family home at Barrells Hall in Warwickshire on an income of £500 a year, forbidden to go within twenty miles of London.

Henrietta pleaded with her husband:

My dearest Life for god sake consider what effect this parting will have, and try to bring yourself to be under the same roof as me for the sake of your Dear Children and what Mr. Knight & his Wife will say; Mama is so good as to wish it, you know how terrible the world's censures are, if you could pass over this you'd ever find me behave as you can desire or direct. I take my solemn oath that this silly but Platonick passion is the only one I have ever had, & yet I now despise my self & the object of it whose face I will never see more nor write to him – Try me for a little while & then if you have the least complaint Ill not so much as endeavour to excuse myself. I am in the most terrible affliction, incapable as yet of shedding tears, if you can be mollified for god's sake endeavour to hide what has passed to the world. If this affair is made publick as you intend, think what tryumph it will be to Mrs. Knight and what affliction to my poor pappa. Do for Heaven's sake don't speak of this & come again to your unfortunate but ever

affectionate H.K I love you better than ever, indeed I do. I
told Mama why I never would consent to what you suspect
me guilty of

Henrietta unsuccessfully tried living in her husband's
London home before opting for the Barrells alternative, her
children placed temporarily in the care of her parents. In spite of
everything, Henrietta made the best of a bad lot, even adopting
the title Lady Luxborough when her estranged husband was raised
to the peerage.

The house at Barrells, situated between Ullenhall and
Henley-in-Arden in Warwickshire had long been neglected and
was in a poor state of repair when Henrietta arrived. In 1739
her cousin Seymour Cholmondeley, the son of her aunt Anne St.
John who had married Thomas Cholmondeley, wrote to Lady
Hertford: 'Her health is bad, and that damn'd wet ditch she's
thrown into, must make it so: that she lives is a miracle, for when
she was sent there were not half the windows up, no doors to the
house, and the roof uncovered.'

Henrietta employed a staff of seven and soon got to work on
the neglected 56-acre Barrells estate. Despite what was considered
a generous allowance from Knight, Henrietta appeared unable to
live within her means and by 1742 was heavily in debt. She had
spent the money left to her by her brother Holles in his will,
selling the family jewels along with her silver plate and dishes.
Knight's advice to her was to halve the number of servants she
employed and get rid of some of her horses.

At some point, Knight must have lifted his ban on writing
materials as Henrietta soon began an extensive correspondence
with her friends and particularly with near neighbour poet
William Shenstone. The communication between Henrietta and
Shenstone began with her response to his work and was written
from Barrells dated Easter Sunday, 1748.

I read your four sonnets with much pleasure; and am obliged
to you for the trouble of transcribing them: they are truly

poetical, yet have an ease as well as delicacy in the turn of thought and expression, which must, I believe, be agreeable to all, whether good judges by their skill and learning, or only judges of good sense and nature. If Dodsley gives a second edition of his well-chosen collection, I hope you will not let your School-mistress [reference to Shenstone's poem written in 1737] be unaccompanied by all her parent's offspring. Now that the boisterous baneful month of March is over, and that the sun resumes his power, I hope, and shall expect to see the productions of your imagination, as much as I shall expect to see those of my parterre, my shrubbery, or grove; and if joined to that satisfaction I have your company here, I shall give double praises to the returning spring.

Henrietta was educated, fluent in French and well-read and her friendship with Shenstone developed first through a love of poetry, but more especially, a love of gardening. Shenstone transformed the family estate at the Leasowes and also became an advocate for the new natural landscape gardening, advising their shared Warwickshire coterie on their own horticultural projects. In time she also entertained other literary luminaries such as William Somerville, Richard Jago and Richard Graves at the renovated Barrells.

And after a silence of some six years, Frances Hertford made contact with Henrietta, who responded immediately. In a letter dated 26 June, 1742 Henrietta wrote to Lady Hertford:

The prospect is a very near one, being surrounded with hills, but is diversified and pretty enough and I have made a garden which I am filling with all the flowering shrubs I can get. I have also made an aviary, and filled it with a variety of singing birds, and am now making a fountain in the middle of it, and a grotto to sit and hear them sing, contiguous to it. This, as it is seen from every window of the house, affords me some amusement. And in a coppice a little farther I have made a very lovely cave shaded by trees.

Henrietta had no contact with her children while they were growing up, and never appeared to have any relationship with her son Henry. Her daughter, however, came back into her life as a newly married young woman and in 1749 Henrietta wrote to Shenstone 'She is now nineteen years old, and I never lay under the same roof with her since she was only 6.'

The young Henrietta Knight was a clever, spirited girl, in character very much like her mother. Like her mother she made an advantageous marriage but looked elsewhere for love. And like her mother became the subject of 18th-century Society gossip when she ran away with a dashing Captain of Dragoons, Josiah Child.

In a letter to Shenstone dated February 2, 1753 Henrietta expresses concern about her daughter in words not dissimilar to those used by others at the time of her own indiscretion:

> My spirits are not only depressed with what affects yours, as solitude, winter storms, and more heavy winter evening but also by the storm my Daughter's imprudence (to call it no worse a name), has raised a storm not only in her family but in the world. This melancholy scene to her friends is I suppose an amusement to the public, and will shortly be a still greater one, who will divert themselves at her and her favourite's expence, whilst her Husband and Friends lament her folly.

During 1749/50 Henrietta planted a lane of white poplars, a lime avenue, and built a ha-ha and a summer house. She planted snowdrops, primroses, polyanthus and violets, which she described as 'the beauties of childhood' – perhaps a reference to Lydiard where the snowdrops continue to flourish.

Until the end of her life Henrietta worked hard in her garden, writing in November 1749 that she had 'stood from Eleven to Five each day in the lower part of my Long Walk, planting and displanting, opening views, etc.'

The woodland snowdrops at Lydiard were a reminder of home for the exiled Henrietta, Lady Luxborough.

But despite the love of her garden and loyal friends, she suffered frequent bouts of depression and towards the end of her life her activities were restricted by the onset of arthritis.

Henrietta lived at Barrells for twenty years and left the house and gardens in a far better condition than she had found them, and when she died her estranged husband couldn't wait to get his hands on the property.

Henrietta died on 26 March, 1756 aged 56. She is buried at St Peter's Church, Wootton Wawen, Warwickshire. Her death warranted a short reference in the newspapers of the day. 'On Tuesday last died the Lady of the Right Hon. Robert Knight, Lord Luxborough, of the Kingdom of Ireland; by whose Death a considerable Fortune descends to the Hon. Joseph [Josiah] Child, Esq: Brother to the Earl of Tylney, who married her only Daughter.'

Horace Walpole, no great admirer of Henrietta, wrote to Lady Ossory in a letter dated 3 August, 1775, some fifteen years after Henrietta's death:

I remember her wearing her little wizen husband's picture in her great black bush of hair: then she fell in love with Parson Dalton for his poetry, and they rhymed together till they chimed – and then I never saw or heard of her any more, till she revived in Mr Shenstone's letters, and was a great performer in his ballad Arcadia. I think these materials promise, considering too that the heroine was sister both of Lord Bolinbroke [sic] and Hollis St John – I expect a mixture of Mrs Eliza Thomas, Machiavel and Shuter.*

Henrietta's letters to William Shenstone were published by J. Dodsley in 1775. James Dodsley worked in partnership with his brother Robert, described as an English bookseller, poet, playwright and miscellaneous writer. Robert was a friend of William Shenstone's and published the poet's work dated 1764-1769. The collection was published with the catchy title – 'Letters from the Right Honourable Lady Luxborough, written with abundant Ease, Politeness, and Vivacity; in which she was scare equalled by any woman of her time. They commenced in the year 1739, and were continued to the year of her death (1756), with some few intermissions.'

Anne Furnese

WHILE SOME OF the Lydiard ladies made little impression upon the house and parkland, Anne Furnese transformed it – or at least her money did.

Anne Furnese was born in about 1711, the daughter of Sir Robert Furnese and his first wife Anne Balam. The Furnese family was fabulously wealthy. Anne's grandfather Sir Henry Furnese, had made a fortune in the hosiery, linen and fine lace business along with a bit of financial wheeling and dealing during the Glorious Revolution of 1688 when he supported King William.

*Elizabeth Thomas was a poet who was said to have turned to prostitution and blackmail in her later years. Edward Shuter was a comedian on the stage at Drury Lane and Covent Garden.

Anne Furnese, first wife of John (Jack) 2nd Viscount St. John whose fortune paid for the remodelling of Lydiard House.

Anne's childhood was spent at the Furnese mansion house at Waldershare in Kent, bought by her grandfather in 1705. The Furnese family were dab hands at remodelling out of date mansion houses and Sir Henry had done a pretty good job on the 17th-century property to designs attributed to William Talman.

John (known as Jack) St. John and Anne Furnese were married at St George's, Hanover Square on 17 April, 1729 and had six children; Frederick, Henry, Louisa and John survived to adulthood, two daughters died young, Ann who died in 1747

The special architectural and historical value of Lydiard House was officially recognised in 1955 when it was awarded a Grade I listing.

aged thirteen and Louisa born in 1740 who died aged just one month old.

The couple's first home was at 51 Brook Street, the footprint of which is now incorporated into the prestigious Claridges hotel. Claridges was built on the site of seven properties numbered 45 – 57 Brook Street constructed between 1723 and 1725. For nearly ten years the couple divided their time between Lydiard, Battersea and Brook Street until in 1738 when Anne, Jack and their young family moved to a new build in South Audley Street, Mayfair. Originally designed by Edward Shepherd as two houses, the St. John's bought both properties for £4,000 and converted them into one.

Sir Robert Furnese had died in 1733 and following the death of his son and heir two years later the Furnese fortune ended up in Chancery where it was eventually divided between Anne and her two sisters. Along with farms and woodland in Kent and the manors of Whitstable and Ellenden, Anne brought at least £20,000 to the Lydiard coffers, worth more than £30 million today. Work began on the Wiltshire estate in about 1738.

A landscaping project and the creation of a new lake saw the parkland transformed. A state-of-the-art Cup and Dome ice house was built in the lakeside woodland, a must-have 18th-century modern convenience. Ice was gathered from the lake and stored packed in layers of straw or reeds in the brick-lined underground pit where it could be expected to last up to eighteen months. Here food was kept fresh for those all-important occasions on the Lydiard social calendar.

The 18th century ice house helped the cook cater for the elaborate entertainments at Lydiard House, including the fashionable new dessert – ice cream.

But despite Anne's considerable inheritance, the remodelling of Lydiard House was constrained by financial restrictions. The original plan was for a much larger building with a fourth tower and two additional facades.

The attainted politician Henry, 1st Viscount Bolingbroke, had been quick to offload the Lydiard estate to his younger half-brother Jack, while retaining many of the financial perks, including the revenue from extensive woodlands in the parishes of Lydiard Tregoze and Lydiard Millicent. At first, he was pleased to know that Jack was going to give the old homestead a makeover. However, when he saw the finished product, he was less enthusiastic.

Little is known about the remodelling of Lydiard House but the favourite candidate for designer is Roger Morris, assistant to popular architect Colen Campbell whose commissions included Wilton House and Longford Castle in Wiltshire. It is thought that Nathaniel Ireson was the builder engaged on the Lydiard project. Henry Cheere is suggested as the sculptor of fireplaces in the Drawing, Dining and State Bedroom, which have features very similar to those in Ditchley Park, the home of Jack's cousin George Henry Lee, Earl of Lichfield.

How much influence did Anne have on how her money was spent? Was she on site when the fixtures and fittings went in? Did she choose the colour scheme? Did she inspect the works, a baby balanced on her hip? The classical decoration in the rooms in the right half of the house, the Dining Room, Drawing Room and State Bedroom is of the Ionic order, the second order of architecture associated with the feminine, so perhaps Anne was consulted on how her home was designed. The Anteroom, now dedicated to the story of Lady Diana Spencer, was created for

The restoration of the 18th century walled garden was central to the Lydiard Park Project in 2004-7.

Anne, a room where she could entertain her female friends and family members. This intimate room contains an extraordinary painted glass window by 17th-century artist Abraham Van Linge and was probably situated in the original house.

When the work was completed, Henry, Viscount Bolingbroke wrote a scathingly critical letter to his half-sister Henrietta saying that Jack and Anne had 'made ymselves a proverb in the country already for their stinginess.'

The house was pretty much finished by 1743 according to a plaque in the attic which reads – 'This House was Rebuilt AD:MDCCXLIII by John Lord Viscount St. John who Married Anne the Daughter & Coheiress of Sr. Robert Furnese Barronet of Waldershare in the County of Kent.' But after all their hard work the couple had scant time to enjoy their new improved country seat. Anne died in July 1747. Following her death Henry offered to help his widowed brother, but perhaps not surprisingly Jack chose to make his own arrangements for his young family.

Writing to Henrietta again Henry said: 'He took no notice of the offer, and I am satisfied with having done what I thought became me.' Henry didn't have a very high opinion of his deceased sister-in-law either, but then he didn't think highly of many people, except himself. 'I wish that the prejudices and habits which his late wife gave him, & which are none of the best, do not stick by him, she had sense and cunning, but I never knew a creature so avaricious, more selfish or more false,' he wrote to Henrietta.

Less than a year after Anne's death Jack remarried. Having suffered poor health throughout his life, Jack embarked upon a restorative trip to Italy with his new wife, only to die in Naples on 26 November, 1748 within four months of his wedding.

Lydiard House is a tribute to Anne Furnese for without her money it is unlikely the remodelling would have taken place. There are also two portraits of her, one in the Drawing Room and one in the State Bedroom. Both paintings picture her in coronation robes. The one featuring her as a younger woman was painted by Isaac Whood, the other by Joseph Highmore.

Hester Clarke

J ACK'S SECOND WIFE Hester Clarke was born in 1723 in
Leominster, Herefordshire, the daughter of wealthy landowner
James Clarke and his wife Frances. There was a connection with
the Knight family and it is possible Hester was introduced to
Jack by Robert Knight, Lord Luxborough, Jack's brother-in-law,
husband of his disgraced sister Henrietta.

Jack made his will on 19 June, 1748, the day he married
Hester Clarke at St Anne's Church, Soho. In August 1748 he
added a Codicil in which he left Hester £1,000 and some personal
items including 'a Sett of Tea China Compleat bought by me at
Bath in June 1748; a Little pearl Neclace of 6 rows small pearl and
a Brilliant Girdle Buckle Square.'

Jack was buried alongside his first wife, Anne in the family
vault in St Mary's, Lydiard Tregoze on 19 March, 1748/9. The
reign of Hester, Lady St. John was a short one. With the death
of Jack, the Lydiard estate and the St. John title passed to his
dissolute son and heir Frederick.

When Hester died in March 1752, she was buried in the
Knight family mausoleum at Barrells, the home to which Jack's
sister Henrietta had been banished.

7

Secrets and Scandals

Lady Diana Spencer

THERE IS A paucity of information about many of the Lydiard Ladies but Lady Diana Spencer has a big story and there is a lot of research material available. Her name appears in numerous historical documents and her life was the subject of relentless gossip exchanged in letters between members of 18th-century society.

Diana Spencer was born on 24 March, 1734 into the illustrious Spencer Churchill family, the great granddaughter of national hero John, 1st Duke of Marlborough and his indomitable wife Sarah. Her father, Charles Spencer, 3rd Duke of Marlborough, was a politician and military commander and her mother was the Hon. Elizabeth Trevor, daughter of Thomas Trevor, 2nd Baron Trevor. The eldest of five children, Diana grew up at Langley Park at Iver, Buckinghamshire, in a house built by her father set in a former medieval deer park landscaped by Lancelot Brown.

While Diana was busy pursuing her artistic hobbies and showing a reluctance to settle down, Frederick St. John had already spent a large portion of the family fortune. Frederick inherited his father's title becoming 3rd Viscount St. John in 1748 when he was just 16 years old and that of 2nd Viscount Bolingbroke after his uncle Henry's death three years later. With estates in Wiltshire, Surrey and Berkshire he had enough disposable income to last most men a lifetime. But Frederick wasn't your average man. The couple met at that notorious party venue Vauxhall Gardens, where wealthy young aristocrats rubbed shoulders with the working girls

*Lady Diana Spencer, wife of Frederick 2nd Viscount Bolingbroke & 3rd
Viscount St. John a study in charcoal by her grandson G.F. St. John after a
portrait by Sir Joshua Reynolds.*

of London. Frederick's companions were teasing him about his
single status when apparently, he turned to Diana and jokingly
asked, 'will you have me?' to which she replied, 'yes, to be sure.'

Following a brief engagement, Frederick and Diana married
on 8 September, 1757 at Harbledon in Kent. Diana brought to
the marriage a £10,000 settlement with an additional £5,000
from her great grandmother Sarah.

The couple made their home at 7 St James' Square, spending
the summer months at Lydiard where Frederick indulged his love

of bloodstock breeding and Diana developed the walled garden, created by her father-in-law.

Their first child, George Richard, was born at the couple's London home on 5 March, 1761 and was christened at St George's, Hanover Square. Their second, a daughter, was born in 1762 when Diana was working long hours in attendance on the Queen. The baby died aged just five months. A second son, Frederick was born on 20 December, 1765.

With Frederick's extravagant lifestyle fast depleting the family finances, Diana used her influence as Lady of the Bedchamber to Queen Charlotte to secure him an appointment as Lord of the Bedchamber to King George III. However, marriage had done little to change Frederick's behaviour and he showed no inclination of curbing his dissolute ways. In 1762 he sold the family pile at Battersea to his wife's cousin, John, Earl Spencer for £30,000 to settle some pressing debts, but this was only the tip of the iceberg. Frederick had the St. John predilection for partying and a large slice of the family fortune had already gone on wine, women and an impressive collection of valuable Sevres porcelain. Along with the thoroughbred racehorses he bought and sold (an estimated 90 during a ten-year period) Frederick also became the patron of George Stubbs, a Lancashire born artist who specialised in painting horses.

By the mid-1760s their marriage had hit the rocks and the Bolingbroke's were merely keeping up appearances, leading pretty much separate lives. Diana moved out of their Lower Brook Street home and placed herself under the protection of her brother George, Duke of Marlborough. A private deed of separation followed Diana's departure in which Frederick agreed to pay her an annual income of £800. Diana cited his violent behaviour and constant drinking.

Now she returned to her other passion – painting. For Diana art was to become much more than just a pleasant pastime, but an important source of income – a career. In 1765 Diana was painted by her mentor, Royal Academician Joshua Reynolds, depicted as a practising artist, indicating the seriousness of her vocation. Diana

During excavation work undertaken in 2004 archaeologists from Wessex Archaeology were able to plot the 18th century paths & flower beds ready for replanting.

was talented and produced a large body of work from designs for the Wedgwood pottery to pastel and watercolour portraits, including one of her second cousin, Georgiana, Duchess of Devonshire, which was later made into an engraving and went into mass production. Horace Walpole commissioned her to produce illustrations of his tragedy *The Mysterious Mother* on seven large panels in black wash mounted on Indian blue damask, which he hung in a specially designed room named the Beauclerc closet in his home at Strawberry Hill.

By 1764 Diana had fallen in love with Topham Beauclerk, a great grandson of Charles II and his mistress Nell Gwyn. However, Diana was soon to discover that what was sauce for the goose was not necessarily sauce for the gander in polite 18th-century society. While it might be acceptable for Frederick to take any number of mistresses, it was certainly not acceptable for Diana to take a lover. And it was crucial that Frederick did not discover she had fallen pregnant. Diana knew that life would be intolerable for her if Frederick sought to make their separation formal. When the child was born even the stained bedsheets were carefully disposed of and the new born baby was immediately sent away. When giving evidence at the divorce trial nurse Mary Molineux, said the child had gone 'to a nurse at some place in or near Westminster.' It was not known whether the child was a girl or a boy or whether it had survived or died.

Of course, once he did find out Frederick immediately instigated divorce proceedings. On 22 January, 1768 he petitioned the House of Lords to bring in a Bill to dissolve his marriage with Lady Diana Spencer on the grounds of her 'criminal conversation' (adultery) with Topham Beauclerk.

The Bolingbroke divorce granted by Act of Parliament was very public and the couple became the subject of society gossip. Diana was forced to resign her position as Queen Charlotte's lady of the bedchamber and to withdraw from public life. The divorce settlement saw Frederick pocket Diana's marriage portion while she was forced to renounce all claims to the Bolingbroke estate. Frederick raised the couple's two sons and Diana saw little of the boys during their childhood. The divorce was issued on 10 March, 1768 and within two days of the divorce receiving royal assent Diana and Topham were married at St George's, Hanover Square on 12 March.

But sadly, Diana's second marriage proved to be little happier than her first. There were three children born of the marriage who survived to adulthood, Mary, Elizabeth and Charles George, but as Beauclerk's laudanum addiction took hold he became increasingly 'morose and savage' and notorious for his lack of personal hygiene.

Frederick ended his days at Lydiard where it was said he suffered both mental and physical ill health and was once described as being 'out of his mind.' He died on 5 May, 1787 and was buried in the family vault at St Mary's, Lydiard Tregoze eight days later.

Following Beauclerk's death in 1780 Diana moved to Spencer Grove, a house at Little Marble Hill, Twickenham where she concentrated on her work. Sadly, her life continued to be plagued by humiliation and heartbreak when in 1787 George Richard, her son by Frederick St. John, engaged in an affair with Mary, her daughter by Topham Beauclerk.

But family life wasn't all scandal and grief for Lady Diana and the *Daily Universal Register* (the forerunner of *The Times*) published on March 29, 1787:

> We cannot but rejoice in the happiness which is to be shared between Lady Pembroke and her sister Lady Diana Beauclerk, on the approaching marriage between the darling son of the one, and the lovely daughter of the other. This match has that sort of foundation, which promises the felicity of all who are connected with it.

Diana's will, written at her Richmond home on 2 August, 1806, includes a number of personal bequests such as a small Alabaster Venus under a glass for Mrs Bouverie (Robert Spencer's mistress) and a miniature portrait of Lord Robert Spencer to go to Lord Bolingbroke (Diana's son) while 'Little Bob' Diana's grandson, the child of her daughter Elizabeth Herbert, received 'all the greenhouse plants.' Diana leaves various pieces of china to her sister Lady Pembroke but then adds 'all other China to Mrs Beauclerk my daughter in law as my Son Charles and Mrs Beauclerk have been kind enough to promise to take care of my dear little Girl (& by this promise will have made my last Moments less terrible).'

The little girl to whom Diana refers is her granddaughter Caroline Mary Jenison, the daughter of Mary Beauclerk who had married Franz 2nd Count Jenison-Walworth in 1796. In 1798 the couple visited Diana in Richmond, leaving with her their eldest child, Caroline Mary, then just a few months old.

In a second codicil written two years later Diana adds: 'If I have at my death any Money either in Cash or Notes I leave it to my Granddaughter Caroline Mary Jenison that is whoever is kind enough to take Charge of her will employ it for her use in whatever way is best for her.'

Ill health and money worries dominated her last years. Depressed and with failing eyesight and tremors of the hand, possibly caused by laudanum, Diana found it impossible to continue to work.

Diana died at her home on 1 August, 1808 aged 74. She was buried at the church of St Mary Magdalene, Richmond on 4 August. The details in the burial register suggest that she was buried in the church, but sadly the site of the grave is now unknown.

Several of Diana's artworks are on display in the Blue Closet in Lydiard House including the Georgiana Cavendish print and an engraving from a drawing of Diana's two daughters, Mary and Elizabeth Beauclerk. Above the fireplace hangs a portrait in pastel of George Richard as a child, drawn by Diana. Three panels depicting ribbons and garlands of flowers painted in gouache and water colour provided useful detail when it came to planting the restored Walled Garden that had once been Diana's inspiration.

The late Diana, Princess of Wales shared an ancestry with Diana Beauclerk and a portrait in the Blue Closet displays a strong family likeness. The charcoal study was drawn by her

The walled garden provided solace for Lady Diana St. John during her trouble marriage and inspiration for her art.

grandson, Rev George Frederick St John copied from a painting by Sir Joshua Reynolds.

Charlotte Collins

GEORGE RICHARD ST. JOHN, 3rd Viscount Bolingbroke, returned to Lydiard House in 1806. He had been away a long time; an awful lot had happened in the intervening years. He had the distinction of marrying bigamously and producing at least fifteen children, of whom only the first three and the last three were legitimate.

George Richard was born on 5 March, 1761 and grew up torn between warring parents Frederick, 2nd Viscount Bolingbroke and his wife Diana. The couple endured an unhappy, volatile marriage that ended in adultery, scandal and eventually a very public divorce in 1768.

The seven-year-old George Richard and his younger brother Frederick were left in the care of their libertine father, hardly the best role model for two young boys. One might have hoped he would have learned a lesson or two from his parents, but it appears George Richard was intent upon making his own mistakes, and plenty of them. Unfortunately, George Richard developed his father's appetites and an attitude of entitlement.

He matriculated at Christ Church College, Oxford on 23 June, 1777 aged 16 but for whatever reason did not graduate. Instead, he moved to Winchester where he was tutored by Rev Thomas Collins, deputy head at Winchester College.

In 1783 George Richard St. John married Charlotte Collins the second daughter of his tutor Rev Thomas Collins. (George later liked to protest that he had been duped into marriage with Charlotte). The ceremony took place in the parish of Compton in Winchester where Charlotte's brother-in-law was the Rector. The entry in the parish register reads:

> February 26, 1783
> By special Licence of his Grace the Archbishop of Canterbury
> the Hon. George Richard St John (elder son of the Lord

Viscount Bolingbroke) & Charlotte Collins second daughter of the Rev. Thomas Collins under-master of Winchester School were married in the Parsonage house between the hours of ten and eleven In the forenoon this twenty sixth day of February one thousand seven hundred and eighty three by me

      Philip Williams Rector of Compton

The witnesses were Charlotte's father and J. Dyson, another of the Rev Collins's pupils.

Of all the indignities inflicted upon the various Lydiard ladies, those suffered by Charlotte St. John must rank as the most iniquitous. Born in about 1760, the middle daughter of three, Charlotte was known by the family nickname Squigg and described by her sister Sally as 'a mouse.' She may have been timid but Charlotte was able to summon reserves of fortitude when abandoned and humiliated by her husband.

The St. John's Battersea estate had been sold to pay for the excesses of his father Frederick and with Lydiard House let to tenants, the couple began their married life in Dorset. Their first child, a son named George, was baptised at the parish church of More Crichel on 4 January, 1784. A daughter Mary was baptised at the same church later that year on 7 December. A second son, Henry, who would later inherit his father's titles and estates, was baptised on 9 March, 1786 at Lytchett Matravers.

And then Mary Beauclerk came to stay.

Mary Beauclerk

MARY WAS THE daughter of Lady Diana Bolingbroke (George Richard's mother) and Topham Beauclerk. Mary's birth was shrouded in secrecy and subterfuge, and believed to have taken place in 1767. Following her mother's divorce from Frederick, 2nd Viscount St. Bolingbroke and her marriage to Topham Beauclerk a second daughter was born. The two girls are frequently referred to as twins, but this is not the case. Elizabeth was born on 19 March, 1769 and baptised on 17 April at St.

George's, Hanover Square. There is no mention of a twin sister baptised on the same day, which would have been the norm. Topham and Diana went on to have a son Charles George born on 20 January, 1774 and baptised in St. Martin in the Fields on 21st February. Further proof that the two girls were not twins is found in the will Topham made on 6 March, 1780 where he described Mary as his eldest daughter. He makes provision for his two younger children should 'my said Son Charles and my Daughter Elizabeth' die before the age of 21, unmarried and without issue.

Mary and her sister Elizabeth had little or nothing to do with their mother's two sons by her first marriage. Then in 1787 Mary paid a visit to her half-brother George Richard and his family, where she clearly forgot her manners.

The couple embarked upon an incestuous relationship and later that same year Mary, accompanied by Charlotte, fled to Paris where she gave birth to a son whom her sister-in-law tried to pass off as her own to avoid yet more family scandal. But the couple's affair soon became common knowledge and the subject of gossip in court circles. Some commentators suggested that George's seduction of his sister was revenge upon his mother for her abandonment of him.

A second son was born a year later and in 1789, pregnant for a third time, Mary, George Richard and their two little sons moved to Paris where the plan was to live in exile and in secret for the rest of their lives. Poor, deluded Mary. After little more than six years and four sons later, George deserted Mary, leaving her living at their bolt hole in Germany where they had removed.

Following the scandal of her husband's desertion and the relationship with his half-sister, Charlotte left Britain with her children and her father. She spent four years living in Italy before she eventually returned to England, but sadly, more heartbreak awaited her. Charlotte's much-loved eldest son George was desperately ill.

Already ill herself, Charlotte had taken lodgings at Clifton, Bristol where she was taking some form of cure. It was from this address that she wrote in a letter to a Miss E. Williams dated 1 July, 1803, just weeks after her son's death.

> but the separation from this belov'd object of my tender care for 19 years stings me to the heart – you my dearest Girls, who knew the irreparable value of what I have lost, will know how impossible it must be, for me to lose the recollection for a moment of his cherubimical angelic countenance. Providence supported me wonderfully in the last trial, I never felt my own debility, & had the resolution never to leave the dear angel 'till He had breathed his last – and I kiss'd his beautiful face every day 'till it was necessary to have his coffin soldered down, don't my dear Girls think that it is any effort to me to write to much upon this subject, I am never easy but when I am talking, or thinking of this Cherubim, & it is only to my prime favourites that I ever mention the subject…

George was buried in the St. John family vault in St Mary's Church, Lydiard Tregoze on 6 June, 1803. Months later Charlotte was staying in Hot Wells, Bristol, where she was taking the waters, but the Lydiard money was in short supply, frittered away on the playthings of the past, dissolute generations. When it came to paying for her own health care, Charlotte was reduced to taking a room in one of the infamous Clifton lodging houses known as 'Death Row.'

Charlotte died on 11 January, 1804 and was buried alongside her son. Her daughter Mary died just four months later. A funerary hatchment was hung by the door at Lydiard House. This painted lozenge shape board displayed Charlotte's coat of arms and included a Latin inscription 'In coelo quio'. The translation of this traditional dictum is 'there is rest in heaven,' which is pretty apt for the cruelly treated Charlotte. The hatchment would have stayed in this position for a year after her death before being transferred to the parish church where it still hangs in the south chapel of St Mary's. Her youngest son Henry inherited the titles 4th Viscount Bolingbroke and 5th Viscount St. John.

But what about Mary Beauclerk, living alone in Germany with four little sons. The resourceful Mary didn't hang about and, perhaps somewhat surprisingly considering she had four illegitimate sons in tow, she found herself a husband in Heidelberg, where George had abandoned her. In 1797 Mary married Francis von Jenison Walworth, Grand Chamberlain of the Household to the King of Wurteemburg and proceeded to have further children.

Apparently, George Richard did not forget Mary or his sons to whom he gave the surname Barton. He might have executed a speedy getaway, but he provided annuities for her and her four sons from the rapidly diminishing Lydiard coffers. And then he took up with Isabella Antoinette, Baroness Hompesch.

So, what happened to the four Barton boys? Charles joined the navy and family folklore has it that he was killed fighting alongside Admiral Nelson. Edward trained as a doctor and settled in Philadelphia. George worked as a Commission Merchant in Boston for Welles & Williams while Robert enjoyed a close relationship with his father.

Mary died on 23 July, 1851 at Heidelberg. She was 84 years old.

A view of the back of Lydiard House taken before work began on the ambitious programme of repair and restoration in the 1950s.

Isabella Charlotte Antoinette Sophia, Baroness Hompesch

I T WOULD APPEAR that while George Richard and Mary were living in Heidelberg, he made the acquaintance of two brothers, Barons Charles and Ferdinand von Hompesch, the sons of Baron Franz Carl Baron von Hompesch and Antonia von Hacke. Invited back to the family's castle at Dusseldorf, George met their young sister Isabella Charlotte Antoinette Sophia von Hompesch. The impressionable seventeen-year-old was seduced by the smooth-talking English aristocrat who conveniently forgot to mention not only Mary and the boys, but his wife Charlotte and the family he had left back home. He persuaded Isabella to marry him in a secret ceremony held in a nearby village church. Then the heartless Lothario threw Isabella's bonnet and shawl in a stream to evince her death by drowning, and later intercepted the girl's letters to her father in which she pleaded for forgiveness for her clandestine marriage.

George Richard brought Isabella to England, but obviously not to his Wiltshire home. Their first son was stillborn in February 1794 in London. A second son, George Frederick, was born the following year, also in London, after which George Richard removed his family to a hideaway in Wales.

Did Isabella never question why they lived a life of secrecy? Why her letters to her family went unanswered? George claimed to be unable to return home as his father Frederick was incensed that he had married a Catholic. Frederick, however, had been dead for more than five years. After two years spent in hiding it would appear that George Richard's cover was blown and the couple left Wales for America. On arriving in New York, the couple first took a house in Greenwich Street where another son William James was born.

In 1798 George Richard bought a property in Elizabethville, New Jersey. Liberty Hall, a 14-room country house standing in 22 acres, was built in 1772 for William Livingstone, a New York lawyer who became Governor of New Jersey and famously signed the American Constitution in 1787 alongside George Washington and Benjamin Franklin. At Liberty Hall George Richard led an undercover existence, known as Lord Bolingbroke to friends only and as Mr Belasise to everyone else. The Rt Hon Augustus John Foster wrote to his mother in September 1805:

> He has been here nearly ten years now, and as they say means to return to England this year. She [Isabella] is anything but handsome; a little square German with broken teeth, but they say very amiable. Their children are remarkably fine. He flatters himself that he is not known here to be Lord Bolingbroke.

Other accounts of Isabella describe her as kind and thoughtful, perhaps unsurprisingly, a resilient character and a woman who found pleasure in everything.

With the death of Charlotte in 1803 George Richard decided to come clean; there is no record of how poor Isabella received the news. So, after a bigamous marriage, six illegitimate children and with Isabella pregnant again, the couple were legally wed on 1 August, 1804 in Trinity Church, New York.

The following year they sold Liberty Hall to wealthy New York City merchant and philanthropist, Thomas Eddy for $12,500 and on 6 June, 1806 the family set sail for England.

Their arrival at Lydiard Park must have set tongues wagging, but then maybe not. By then George Richard's reputation was well known. His mother Lady Di wrote to Mary 'G and Lady B are living at Lydiard, the people round them are very civil and visit them, – in this part of the world it is very different.'

Isabella had eleven children of whom three sons were stillborn. John Jeremiah Dyson was born at Lydiard House on 28 September, 1810 where he died on 15 June, 1812. A segment of his memorial stone has at some point been re-used to pave the church path and can be seen close to the west door. Isabella's two daughters, both born in America, also died young. Isabella left a record of the death of both of them. 'Dearest Angelic Isabella died April 24th 1822 at Richmond in consequence of fright after

14 days illness & at last Brain fever. A Seraph's eye a Seraph's Soul was hers.' In 1826 her daughter Antonia died in Paris. Isabella recorded 'lost my heart's comfort.'

George's last years were dogged by ill health. It was he who built the plunge pool on the edge of the lake in Lydiard Park in 1820, revealed during excavations in 2005 ahead of the parkland restoration project.

In 1824 he left Lydiard with his daughter for a restorative tour of Italy. He died in Pisa on 11 December, 1824. His body was returned for burial in the family vault at St Mary's.

Isabella outlived her husband by more than twenty years. At the time of the 1841 census, she was living in Torquay, close to her eldest son George who was a vicar there.

Among the bequests in her will dated 4 July, 1848 Isabella left £15 to the priests of the Bavarian Chapel in Warwick Street, Westminster to pay for a Requiem Mass with organ and voices. She bequeathed a further £10 for the priests to distribute amongst the 'poor old Germans' who attend the chapel. Back home at Lydiard she left £40 to her Bailiff Henry Eveleigh and £10 to his wife. She also left Bailiff Eveleigh £15 to distribute to the 'poor old people at Lydiard.' Among the personal items she gave 'to the present Lord Harry Viscount Bolingbroke the portrait of his late father my husband painted by his mother Lady Diana when a child.' This portrait is 'to be hung in the drawing room at Lydiard as before.'

Isabella Charlotte Antoinetta Sophia Viscountess Bolingbroke died at Torquay and was buried on 22 July, 1848 in the St. John family vault alongside her husband, George Richard and his first wife Charlotte.

8

Hard Times

Lady Mary Emily Elizabeth St. John

IN 1881 THE population of the parish of Lydiard Tregoze numbered 660. The tenant farmers paid their rent to the estate steward and every summer Henry, Viscount Bolingbroke returned to Lydiard Park for the shooting season. In this small, close knit community everyone knew everyone else's business. It is unlikely his Lordship's shenanigans went unnoticed.

There's a romantic story about how Henry, 5th Viscount Bolingbroke and Mary Howard first met, involving a horse that cast a shoe, a visit to a blacksmith and a chance meeting. Was this a story invented by the love-struck lord, or the young woman whose reputation was ruined? The truth is probably a tad more mundane.

Mary Emily Elizabeth Howard was born on 31 January, 1859 in the neighbouring village of Lydiard Millicent, the eldest child of Robert Howard, gardener, carter and sometime blacksmith, and his wife Susanna the daughter of Robert Hiscock, gamekeeper at Lydiard Park. By 1871 Mary was living in the gamekeeper's cottage, cared for her by her grandparents. She would have been no stranger to Henry.

By 1882 Henry 62, and the 23-year-old domestic servant were living at an address in Bath where a son, Henry Mildmay was born. Perhaps it should be mentioned here that at this time Henry was still involved with Ellen Medex, a woman he would later claim to be his wife and by whom he had a daughter, Ellen Rose. Perhaps Henry had qualities that are not immediately obvious now, more than 140 years later.

Photograph of Lady Mary Emily Elizabeth St. John, the wife of Henry Mildmay St. John 5th Viscount Bolingbroke & 6th Viscount St. John.

In 1885 Mary had a second son Charles Reginald. The story continues that when the couple visited Lydiard Park, Mary would resume her role as housekeeper while the children remained in Bath with their nursemaid. However, photographs held in the Lydiard archives show Henry, Mary and one of the boys captured in front of Lydiard House, so maybe this is another story without foundation.

By 1893 Mary was pregnant again and Henry eventually got around to marrying her. The ceremony took place in the Bath Registry Office on 5 January, 1893. A daughter was born soon after but the child did not survive.

Following the death of Ellen Medex in 1885, Henry engaged in a war of words with the editor of *Debrett's Peerage*. He insisted that his entry be altered to include the death of his wife, Ellen whom he stated he had married in 1869 and their two sons (Mary's sons) the Hon. Henry Mildmay, born in 1880 and the Hon Charles Reginald born in 1883. How could Mary have forgiven Henry for his appalling treatment of her?

The editor Arthur G.M. Hesilrige, requested a marriage certificate and birth certificates for the two boys to which an indignant Henry replied that his word was enough. However, it wasn't for Mr Hesilrige and the marriage details and the birth of Henry's sons were omitted from Debrett.

Henry died at his Lydiard home on 7 November, 1899, aged 79. His funeral took place at St Mary's Church, where, following the service Henry's solicitor handed a statement to the two journalists who were in attendance. Mary revealed her marriage to Henry had taken place six years earlier and introduced their three-year-old son Vernon. There appears to be no mention of the couple's two older illegitimate sons.

Did this come as a huge surprise to the Lydiard Tregoze villagers? It certainly did to Henry's cousin Canon Maurice William Ferdinand St. John who believed himself to be the heir to the Lydiard titles and estates.

Mary could have been under no illusions as to the state of the Lydiard Estate affairs. There had been little or no maintenance on the Palladian mansion house since the 18th-century remodelling project and the farms were all in the hands of mortgagees. Maybe the Canon St. John had a lucky escape?

So, Mary brought her boys home and settled into her role as Lady of the Manor. She assumed her duties as Lady Bolingbroke with the help of her cousin Edward Hiscock whom she created Estate Manager. From all accounts she was a kind, approachable woman who took her obligations seriously, despite the huge financial constraints placed upon her.

In 1920, with the estate mortgaged to the hilt and the once elegant mansion house in disrepair, Mary sold off 1,000 acres of farmland. By the 1930s a large part of Lydiard House was uninhabitable and it was said in some rooms the four poster beds were supporting the ceilings while holes in the roof could be clearly seen.

A second property sale followed in March 1930 when the local press announced that 'for economic reasons Lady Bolingbroke decided to dispose of her estate at Lydiard.' Described as one of the largest sales held in Swindon for many years it was reported that 'attractive offers have been received for the purchase of the estate as a whole, but it was Lady Bolingbroke's desire that her tenants should have an opportunity of securing their holdings.'

Mary spent the last years of her life in poverty and bedridden in a small room overlooking the church path where, it was said, she was able to see people coming and going to church on Sundays.

Lady Bolingbroke died on 22 February, 1940 and was buried alongside her husband in the new vault in the churchyard at St Mary's, Lydiard Tregoze. Mourners included her three sons, Edward Hiscock and the tenants and estate workers with whom she had grown up. Among the floral tributes were cards signed 'in affectionate remembrance, from all at Windmill Farm' and 'With loving sympathy from children and teachers at Lydiard Tregoze school.'

Her cousin, Mr William Hiscott [Hiscocks] aged sixty-nine, smallholder, of Lydiard Millicent, and gamekeeper on the estate, told a reporter from the *Bath Chronicle and Weekly Gazette*:

Lady Bolingbroke's mother was my father's sister. My father was gamekeeper here and she came to live with us. We were brought up together by my grandmother. She went into service at Lydiard Park, grew up a tall, fine woman and became housekeeper. The first we knew of her marriage was after the funeral. She and her baby son, the young heir, then went to live at the Park. It made no difference between us. She never took on airs because of her position, and we often visited her, although, of course, we were her servants.

Interestingly he too made no mention of Mary's two elder sons.

Mary's death marked the beginning of the end of the St. John inheritance at Lydiard Park. Her will, unaltered since she made it in 1902, left the estate to be held in trust for her son Vernon, naming her solicitor and Edward Hiscock as trustees. An article published in the *North Wilts Herald* in March 1941 reported that Lady Mary 'left estate of the gross value of £16,492, with net personality £1,936 2*s* 4*d*'. The St. John wealth had long since gone to pay for the dissolute excesses of previous generations. In 1943 the remaining farms and land in the two parishes of Lydiard Tregoze and Lydiard Millicent were sold. Finally, the mansion house and 147 acres of parkland were bought by Swindon Corporation.

Ellen Rose St. John

WHILE LADY BOLINGBROKE lived her last years under huge financial constraints on the Lydiard Park estate, her step-daughter Ellen Rose St. John was living in poverty in rented rooms in Croydon, Surrey.

On a cold, wet November day in 1899 Ellen Rose St. John followed the funeral procession into St. Mary's Church of her father, Henry Mildmay St. John, Viscount Bolingbroke. The inscription on the wreath she laid at her father's grave read 'Dearest Father, deepest grief, Dolly.' She uses an affectionate childhood name but it is impossible to know how close the two had been during her father's last years when Ellen had lived on the periphery of Henry's life. Ellen Rose was the only surviving child born to Ellen Medex and Henry Mildmay St. John, 5th Viscount Bolingbroke, during a clandestine relationship lasting more than 30 years.

Henry Mildmay St. John, described as an 'eccentric' child, grew up to have a very secretive personality. He succeeded to the titles of 5th Viscount Bolingbroke, 6th Viscount St. John, Baron St. John of Lydiard Tregoze and Baron St. John of Battersea in 1851 and soon after met Ellen Medex. He was 31 years old and she was seventeen. It was said that he proposed marriage to the young girl within days of their first meeting, but thwarted by her sister, the couple eloped to Holland.

Henry and Ellen led a nomadic lifestyle, spending several years living abroad. On their return to London, they lived at various addresses under the alias Mr and Mrs Morgan, but despite Henry's subsequent protests, it appears extremely doubtful that the couple ever wed. Ellen had a son who died at birth and a daughter, Ellen Rose. Ellen Rose once commented that she did not know her exact date of birth. However, an entry in the parish registers of St. Marylebone, Westminster records a baptism for Ellen Rosa St. John the daughter of Henry and Ellen Morgan, 19 Upper Baker Street on 27 June, 1862.

Ellen Medex died in 1885 and was buried in Highgate Cemetery, her coffin plate inscribed 'Ellen, Viscountess Bolingbroke.' After her death Henry assumed the mantle of grieving widower, but all was not as Henry would have liked the London society gossips to believe. By the time of Ellen's death, he was already involved with his housekeeper Bessie Howard who had two sons by him.

At the time of the 1891 census Ellen Rosie St. John aged 29 occupied four rooms at 39 Cornwall Road close to Waterloo Station with her companion Minnie Breton, where she lived on an income of private means, most probably money left to her by her mother. By 1911 she was living in a six roomed flat at 11 Babington Road, Streatham where she employed a maid Minnie Leonard.

Difficult to locate on the Victorian census returns, Ellen could have become a mere footnote in the St. John family history if it

were not for a handful of letters in the St. John family papers held
by the Wiltshire and Swindon History Centre in Chippenham.
The surviving letters date from the 1930s when Ellen Rose, then
in her late sixties, lived at 13 Malvern Road, Thornton Heath,
Surrey and are addressed to Harold Dale at H. Bevir & Son, the
St. John family solicitors.

On May 25 (no year) she writes:

> Dear Mr Dale,
> I am writing this to ask you if Lady Bolingbroke is still at
> Lydiard as I have written to her & as she has not answered my
> letters I wondered if she received them. She always sent my
> rent Ch. Through Mr Goodwin & I have not had any cheque
> this month (due 11th) I don't think he can realize what that
> means to me.

Mr Dale's reply does not survive with Ellen's letters, but he
has obviously tried to explain that Lady Bolingbroke also battled
financial hardship, the consequences of the extravagances of
previous generations of the St John family. On May 28 Ellen Rose
writes again.

> Dear Mr Dale,
> Thank you for letter. Indeed I don't know what to do. This
> calamity has come so suddenly & I have this little house
> which is rented at only £5 p. month & one has to <u>live</u> as
> well. My sight is too bad to do any eyesight work & I am
> dependent on the amount sent from Lydiard. I had <u>no</u> idea
> things were so bad, as if I had known, I might have been able
> to have sold my small amount of furniture & gone to another
> place. I have been here 30 years & the case in the House of
> Lords simply ruined me here as people here have never been
> the same to me.
> I think I have worried you with enough of my troubles.
> I only hope I may be able to pay my way – everything is so
> dear in the way of rent – only two rooms are £1.5 !!! I am

trying to let mine, <u>but bad luck</u> seems to be the order of the day.

> With Kind regards
> Sincerely Yrs
> E. St John

The case in the House of Lords to which Ellen Rose refers was when Vernon Henry St. John, her father's only legitimate son, petitioned the government for the titles due to him. The subsequent hearing received extensive press coverage and exposed the details of Henry's love affairs and subterfuge.

The account published in the *Bath Chronicle and Weekly Gazette* on April 17, 1926 reported all the lurid details:

> From 1869 to 1885 he lived in London with a Miss Medex as Mr and Mrs Morgan, and had one daughter, but it was alleged that they were never married. In her death certificate the Viscount described her as his wife, but no record of the marriage could be found. In a report the Attorney General said that two other sons were born to the Viscount and Viscountess, who lived for many years at Bath before their marriage as Mr and Mrs Wilson. It was stated that neither of these sons made any claim to the title. It was alleged that Lord Bolingbroke did not register the births of these sons, neither of whom claimed the peerage. Counsel contended there was no evidence of male issue from Medex and that petitioner was entitled to a writ of summons. Claimant alleged that there was no marriage between the late Viscount and Ellen Medex. They had one child, who survived infancy, a daughter, and it was alleged that the Viscount married for the first time, in 1893, Mary Howard, by whom after marriage he had one son only, the claimant born in 1896. The report of the Attorney-General said there was no considerable evidence that the Viscount and Ellen Medex were married in 1887. He wrote to certain peerage publications that he had been married to Ellen Medex, and that there had been issue, Henry Mildmay, born in 1880, and Charles, born in 1883. It was

probable, declared the report, that they were not sons of Ellen Medex, but of the late Viscount by Miss Howard, before their marriage. They lived at Bath under the name of Wilson, and had two sons Henry Mildmay and Charles Reginald.

Poor Ellen Rose!

Perhaps the worry of it all caused her to forget she had already written to Mr Dale, because on May 29 she writes yet again, concluding:

I hope Lady Bolingbroke is fairly well under these trying circumstances.

A letter dated July 1 is written in a somewhat sterner tone.

Dear Mr Dale,

What do you think I can exist upon? The Vicar, & Dr think it a most cruel & dreadful thing not to send me <u>anything</u>. The <u>family</u> cannot believe such a thing. My Father <u>not</u> being on friendly terms with them has made it bad for me. Surely there could be a little after so many years & at my time of life & with my Broncheal Asthma it would be impossible for me to get anything to do & it came so suddenly. I hope you will try to send me something

Yr truly E. St John.

Harold Dale replies to Ellen Rose in a letter dated July 3, 1930, again trying to explain Lady Bolingbroke's situation.

Dear Miss St. John,

I am really awfully sorry for you, and do appreciate the position you are in – but Lady Bolingbroke is in exactly the same position, and has no income whatever.

She also does not know what to do, and she has such heavy expenses in connection with the house and there is nothing to meet them with.

The position with regard to the future is still in the balance and a great deal depends upon whether any further sales of land take place.

At the moment the mortgagees will require the whole income and Lady Bolingbroke is powerless in the matter.

It is a most terrible situation for you.

Meanwhile Ellen Rose applied to a charitable society to ask for help but on 12 July she writes again to Harold. Still apparently unappreciative of Lady Bolingbroke's situation she reveals a little of her father's autocratic attitude:

> I cannot understand how it is that Lydiard has got into that terrible state. Lady Bolingbroke could let part of the house & people bring their own servants. That, would bring her in a little. I have had an old Lady here for some years paying 10/- & that small sum helped. She has had a bad mental illness & I nursed her & did my own work as well & was obliged to give up as it was far too much for me & now the rooms are empty. I do wish I could let them. The upper part. I hope you are keeping well. The weather is so lovely now
> With kind regards
> Yrs sincerely E. St John.

You have to have some sympathy for poor Mr Dale caught between these two elderly women, both in dire straits.

Ellen Rose kept up the pressure until on 23 December, 1931 Lady Bolingbroke wrote to Harold.

> Dear Mr Dale,
> In reply to your letter with reference to Miss St. John's letter to you. I am enclosing a cheque for five pounds made out to you as I think it advisable it should be sent to her from you.
> Yours sincerely,
> Mary E.E. Bolingbroke

Sadly, Ellen Rose's eventual rescue might have come at the expense of Lady Mary's death in 1940. In her will dated 1902

Mary's first bequest was an annuity of £100 per annum to Ellen St. John. However, a letter dated 3 June, 1942 from Bevir's to the Estate Duty Office in Llandudno states that owing to the condition of the Lydiard estate there was not sufficient income to pay the annuities, much less the duties.

Following the death of Lady Bolingbroke, Bevir's engaged a Mr T. Johnston to ascertain if Ellen Rose was still alive. In his report he describes her as a lady about 75 years of age who said her name was St. John, which she pronounced as "Sin Jean". He wrote:

> The person I saw was somewhat refined in manner about 5 feet 6 in height, medium build, and had dark greyish hair. She was very sharp in her answers and appeared to be a reticent person. There is no doubt, but that she is identical with the lady, the subject of your enquiry.

Ellen died in the Mayday Hospital Croydon in March 1942. D.H. Ebbutt Ltd Funeral Directors and Monumental Masons of Purley invoiced Bevir's with a covering letter.

> To Waxed and Polished Coffin: Brass Furnishings: Plate engraved with Inscription.
>
> To Rolls Royce Hearse and Bearers: Attending Mayday Hospital: Attending Service Croydon Cemetery.
>
> To Cemetery fees paid on your behalf.
>
> To Non-Conformist Ministers's Fee.
>
> Total £25 8s od

> Dear Sirs,
>
> We have this day conducted the Funeral of the late Ellen St John, Aged 79 Years, who died in Mayday Hospital, Croydon, Surrey.
>
> The Non-Conformist Service was conducted in the Cemetery Chapel; the Interment was in a Private Grave in The Croydon Cemetery, Mitcham Road, Croydon, Grave No. 20642 Plot F.5.

> We have paid the Cemetery Fees on your behalf and as
> no grave can be purchased in the Croydon Cemetery without
> a Registered Owner, and the Mayday Hospital Officials could
> give us no names of relatives, we purchased this grave in the
> registration of yourselves; and if you know of any relatives,
> then, of course, you could Re-register this grave in their name.

No jewellery was found in her squalid rooms, just a lot of old clothes and a few bits of china along with a model of a Chinese Junk in a glass case described as 'pretty.' Croydon Borough Council took into safe keeping a few items of silver plate; some spoons and forks, an entrée dish, two salvers, a sauce boat and a dressing table set, all of which later proved to be of no value.

Communications survive between the Mayday Hospital, Croydon Borough Council and the St. John solicitors in Wootton Bassett where Bevir's claim to have heard nothing about Ellen Rose for twenty years. What had happened to the 1930s correspondence between her and Mr Dale?

Ellen Rose had rented her two rooms from a Miss/Mrs L. Lavery at 10s 6d per week and by 7 September, 1942 the landlady was anxious to receive the back dated rent owed to her. When she visited the property some months after Ellen Rose's death she was horrified at the condition of the rooms, writing to Bevir's that 'Mice jump out of the drawers.' It can only be hoped that things were not that bad when Ellen Rose was living there.

An examination of her financial affairs revealed that at the time of her death Ellen Rose had less than £2 in her bank account and had been receiving a small pension from St Monica's, Bristol. Poor Ellen Rose's posthumous financial dilemma now became Lord Bolingbroke's and for the first time in his life he was forced to acknowledge his responsibilities towards his half-sister.

But neither Lord Bolingbroke nor Bevir's acting on his behalf wanted anything to do with the matter of clearing up Ellen Rose's estate. In all fairness to them they had rather a lot on their plate with the Lydiard Park estate about to go on the market. Lord Bolingbroke wrote to Mr Dale: 'Many thanks for your letter &

for inquiring into the affairs you mention. I note all you say & can only presume that the Local Authorities in question were entitled to take possession of the articles described & that the remaining miscellany towards the rent due?'

Unlike Lady Bolingbroke whose funeral two years previously was attended by family, friends, tenants and estate workers at the St Mary's parish church in Lydiard, Ellen Rose St John was laid to rest in Croydon Cemetery. It seems unlikely anyone other than the funeral director and the Minister attended her burial.

9

The Last Lydiard Lady

Two of the last ladies to live in Lydiard House were Joyce Gough and Joyce Ingram, but neither of them were members of the St. John family nor of the aristocracy.

Joyce Gough

When Swindon Corporation acquired Lydiard House and Park in 1943, they were quick to appoint a caretaker. The empty mansion house proved an irresistible attraction for the American soldiers stationed at the military camp. The soldiers broke into both the mansion and St Mary's Church, stealing the Communion wine and causing damage in the house. Their misdemeanour resulted in a dressing down by the Rector to a full congregation in the church. But the local authority wasn't going to risk the same thing happening again and Harry Gough, the verger at St Mary's, was appointed caretaker and moved in with his wife Phyllis and their two daughters, Joyce and Phyllis Joan. The family lived in the former servants' quarters where conditions were pretty basic – just one toilet and no electricity.

Although the State Rooms were empty and the house was in a poor condition, the Gough family led guided tours for small groups of visitors and their daughter Joyce had fond memories of living there, despite her initial reservations. She would later write about her experiences of moving into the dilapidated mansion.

> The first night I thought my father was the most cruel person on earth taking us there because there were no conveniences, we had candles and Aladdin oil lamps and instead of a cooker

mother had to use what was known as a Triplex. It was like
a fireplace with an oven to one side. The downstairs wasn't
too bad but the upstairs was in a terrible state. I don't think
there was a bedroom ceiling that didn't have a huge hole in it
somewhere. You could look through right up into the attic.

Harry Gough retired and the couple moved out in the mid-1950s,
just before Lydiard House was opened to the public. Joyce wrote:

> However, I must confess the first time I returned I resented
> so many people being there, and yes, it was a little selfish of
> me, but I remembered Lydiard Park with just my father and
> my mother, sitting on a seat on the front lawn – with the
> daffodils out, they both so adored living there. It was silly
> really, I couldn't stand in the way of progress.

Joyce Ingram

NORMAN AND JOYCE Ingram found the staff accommodation
much improved when they became caretakers and moved
into Lydiard House in 1967 with a spacious two bedroomed
apartment overlooking the parkland.

Joyce took over as full-time caretaker following the death of
her husband in 1975, a post she held until she retired in 1991.
In an interview published in the *Swindon Advertiser* on 15 April,
1989 Joyce told of her love for her job, Lydiard House and an
apparition of Sir John St. John 1st Baronet, whose presence she
frequently encountered when going about her duties.

Joyce told the *Swindon Advertiser*: 'You can always tell when
he's around. The temperature drops dramatically, I get goose
pimples and sometimes he has a distinctive and sickly smell. It
could be the smell of decay I suppose. He's been dead since 1648.'

In 1982 Joyce was pictured in the *Thamesdown News*
welcoming home the Peter Lely portrait of Barbara, Countess of
Castlemaine, Charles II's notorious mistress and Barbara St. John's
granddaughter. The portrait was sold by Vernon, 6th Viscount
Bolingbroke along with others following the sale of the estate in

1943, but was bought back by Thamesdown Borough Council with additional funding from the Victoria and Albert Museum and the National Heritage Memorial Fund.

The State Rooms were then open to the public 10-1 and 2-5.30 weekdays, Saturdays and Bank Holidays and 2-5.30 on Sundays, admission free. Joyce worked a 42-and-a-half-hour week, greeting visitors, serving in the gift shop and cleaning the rooms.

Joyce was not looking forward to retirement and feared that Thamesdown Borough Council would rehouse her in 'a poky little place.'

In the May 1991 edition of the *Friends of Lydiard Tregoz Report* No. 24, Sarah Finch-Crisp, Keeper at Lydiard House, wrote:

> Joyce has been with us many years and has become virtually an institution. Her love for Lydiard and for the people who visit it has always been paramount, and her commitment to the Museum's service, never in doubt. We and many other will miss her friendliness, efficiency and her devotion to duty. *Au revoir*, Joyce – see you soon.

Joyce Ingram, the last of the Ladies of Lydiard.

Acknowledgements

I WOULD LIKE to acknowledge the work of the late Canon Brian Carne without whom this book would not have been written.

Brian Carne served as Rector of Lydiard Millicent with Lydiard Tregoz from 1960-1968. His research into the history of St. Mary's, Lydiard House and Park and the St. John family became his great passion and although he eventually moved on it was as if he never left.

With Frank Smallwood, a former master at Sir Walter St. John's School in Battersea, Brian founded the Friends of Lydiard Tregoz (the precursor of the Friends of Lydiard Park). For forty years he edited and contributed articles to the Friends of Lydiard Tregoz Reports, a scholarly publication published annually and deposited at prestigious repositories such as the British Library, the Bodleian Library and the College of Arms. Everything you could ever want to know about the Lydiard Estate can be found in this vast body of work. In addition to this Brian wrote 'Curiously Painted' the story of the unique St. John polyptych in St Mary's Church.

Sadly, I only met Brian once at a Friends' annual meeting. He showed me a brick discovered beneath the St. John tomb during an earlier restoration project. The 17th-century brick was one of many found beneath the chapel floor supporting the alabaster memorial above, and was probably made on site at Lydiard Park. We both marvelled at the brick which bore the imprint of the brickmakers finger in the clay. I exchanged several letters with Brian and whenever I told him about some exciting discovery I had made, he was equally excited for me, never mentioning that he had found the same information many years previously.

I should also like to thank Sonia St. John who has always been unfailingly supportive, patient and encouraging. Sonia, an expert on the history of the St. John family, kindly read the early chapters of this book, putting me straight on the birthplace of Oliver St. John.

Thank you also to Elizabeth St. John, who despite being a bit busy writing three hugely successful historical novels – The Lydiard Chronicles – always found time to encourage and support my work as well.

My thanks go to Sarah Finch-Crisp, for so many years Keeper at Lydiard House, who now works in a voluntary capacity as Chair of the Friends of Lydiard Park. Her knowledge and enthusiasm for all things Lydiard is inexhaustible.

My thanks go to the curatorial team at Lydiard House who have kindly allowed me to use images of the portraits of the lovely Ladies of Lydiard.

Although I have done my homework, any errors that occur are mine alone.

Bibliography

Aston, Mark, 'The St. John's Huguenot Connection', *Friends of Lydiard Tregoz Report No. 40* (May 2007), pp. 3-8.

Bannister, Rev. A.T., *The History of Ewias Harold, its castle, priory, and church*. (The Bible and Crown Press, 1902).

Bowler, Sidney D.A., 'Lydiard Park Camp', *Friends of Lydiard Tregoz Report No. 16* (May 1983), pp. 14-16.

Brown, Jane, *My Darling Heriott – Henrietta Luxborough, Poetic Gardener and Irrepressible Exile*. (Harper Press, 2006).

Carne, Canon Brian (ed.), 'Five Letters of Anne, Countess of Rochester', *Friends of Lydiard Tregoz Report No. 6* (May 1973) pp. 18-23.

Carne, Canon Brian (ed.), 'The St. John Vault', *Friends of Lydiard Tregoz Report No. 18* (May 1985) pp. 28-34.

Carne, Canon Brian, 'Frederick, 1732-87, 2nd Viscount Bolingbroke, 3rd Viscount St. John', *Friends of Lydiard Tregoz Report No. 21* (May 1988) pp. 15-39.

Carne, Canon Brian (ed.), 'Funeral of Henry Mildmay St. John, 5th Viscount Bolingbroke', *Friends of Lydiard Tregoz Report No. 24* (May 1991) pp. 20-21.

Carne, Canon Brian, 'St. John Papers 1', *Friends of Lydiard Tregoz Report No. 27* (May 1994) pp. 41-102.

Carne, Canon Brian, 'St. John Papers Part 2', *Friends of Lydiard Tregoz Report No. 28* (May 1995) pp. 55-98.

Carne, Canon Brian, 'John, 2nd Viscount St. John (1702-1748)', *Friends of Lydiard Tregoz Report No. 33* (May 2000) pp. 29-51.

Carne, Canon Brian, 'The Decline and Fall of the St. Johns of Lydiard Tregoze', *Friends of Lydiard Tregoz Report No. 34* (May 2001) pp. 34-55.

Carne, Canon Brian, 'Some More St. John Family Papers', *Friends of Lydiard Tregoz Report No. 37* (May 2004) pp. 31-58.

Carne, Canon Brian, 'Notes on the Fabric and Fittings of St. Mary's Church and Related Matters', *Friends of Lydiard Tregoz Report No. 38* (May 2005) pp. 5-39.

Carne, Canon Brian (ed.), 'An Architect for Lydiard Park', *Friends of Lydiard Tregoz Report No. 38* (May 2005) pp. 72-75.

Carne, Canon Brian, 'George Richard (1761-18240, 3rd Viscount Bolingbroke and his families', *Friends of Lydiard Tregoz Report No.*

39 (May 2006) pp. 29-46.

Carne, Canon Brian, *Curiously Painted – An illustrated history of the St. John family polyptych at Lydiard Tregoze*. (Friends of Lydiard Park, 2007).

Clarendon, Edward Hyde Earl of, 1674, *Characters of eminent men in the reigns of Charles I and II*. (R. Faulder, 1793).

Cooper, Charles Henry, 1840, *Memoire of Margaret, Countess of Richmond and Derby*. (Deighton Bell & Co., 1874).

Crittall, Elizabeth (ed.), *A History of the County of Wiltshire* (Victoria County History Vol. 9) pp.75-90.

Domvile, Lady Margaret, *Memoir of Margaret Beaufort, Countess of Richmond and Derby*. (Burns & Oates, London).

Eastman, Michael, 'Monument to Sir John St. John, First Baronet, and his Two Wives, 1634', *Friends of Lydiard Tregoz Report No. 12* (May 1979) pp. 41-49.

Erskine, Mrs Steuart, *Lady Diana Beauclerk Her Life and Work* (T. Fisher Unwin, 1903).

Fisher, Kevin, *Lydiard Park: The last 75 Years*. (Lydiard Park Heritage Trust, 2018).

Gingell, P.J. and S.T. Ball, 'Midgehall', *Friends of Lydiard Tregoz Report No. 11* (May 1978) pp. 1-9.

Gray, Michael, 'Lydiard Park, Wiltshire – Analysis and Architectural Assessment of a Palladian Country House', *Friends of Lydiard Tregoz Report No. 33* (May 2000) pp. 3-13.

Harris, William, *An Historical and Critical Account of the Lives and Writings of James I and Charles I and the lives of Oliver Cromwell and Charles II From Original Writers and State Papers*. (F.C. and J. Rivington, 1814).

Hicks, Carola, *Improper Pursuits the Scandalous Life of Lady Di Beauclerk*. (Macmillan, 2001)

Hopkinson, M.R., *Married to Mercury*. (Constable & Co. Ltd., 1936).

Hymers, J. B.D. (ed.), *The Funeral Sermon of Margaret Countess of Richmond and Derby – Preached by Bishop Fisher in 1509*. (Cambridge University Press, 1860).

Jacob, William L., 'Lord of the Turf', *Friends of Lydiard Tregoz Report No. 21* (May 1988) pp. 40-46.

Jones, Michael K. and Malcolm Underwood, *The King's Mother Lady Margaret Beaufort Countess of Richmond and Derby*. (Cambridge University Press, 1992).

Lambert, David, 'Lydiard Park – Swindon's own Arcadia', *Friends of Lydiard Tregoz Report No. 27* (May 1994) pp. 28-30.

Lane, Dr. Joan, 'Lady Luxborough and Her Garden', *Friends of Lydiard Tregoz Report No. 36* (May 2003) pp. 31-36.

Leighton, Gerard, 2002, 'The East Window of Lydiard Tregoze Church', *Friends of Lydiard Tregoz Report No. 35* (May 2002) pp. 27-31.

Letters written by the Late Right Honourable Lady Luxborough to William Shenstone, Esq. (J. Dodsley, 1775).

Marshall, Nell, 'Henrietta's Story', *Friends of Lydiard Tregoz Report No. 36* (May 2003) pp. 7-30.

Newton, Stella Mary, 'Dress and Fashion in the Portraiture at Lydiard Tregoz,' *Friends of Lydiard Tregoz Report No. 21* (May 1988) pp. 1-10.

Ormond, Richard, 'Portraits at Lydiard Tregoze', *Friends of Lydiard Tregoz Report No. 5* (May 1972) pp.1-10.

Pearson Associates, Nicholas, 'Extracts from the Report on the Park at Lydiard Tregoze', *Friends of Lydiard Tregoz Report No. 37* (May 2004) pp. 3-23.

Phillips, Bernard, 'An archaeological Evaluation in the Walled Garden at Lydiard Park, Lydiard Tregoze, (SU10278485)', *Friends of Lydiard Tregoz Report No. 35* (May 2001) pp. 5-25.

Royale, Trevor, *The Road to Bosworth Field.* (Little Brown, 2009).

Sergeant, Philip W., *My Lady Castlemaine Being a Life of Barbara Villiers Countess of Castlemaine, afterwards Duchess of Cleveland.* (Hutchinson, 1912).

Smallwood, F.T., 'Henry St. John the Elder and the Estcourt Murder', *Friends of Lydiard Tregoz Report No. 5* (May 1972), pp. 22-59.

Smith, Charlotte Fell, *Mary Rich, Countess of Warwick (1625-1678) Her Family & Friends.* (Longmans, Green & Co., 1901).

Stirling, A.M. Wilhelmina, 1956, *The Merry Wives of Battersea and Gossip of Three Centuries.* (Robert Hale Ltd., 1956).

Taylor, John George, *Our Lady of Batersey.* (George White, 1925)

Documents, newspapers and websites

Macgregor, John E.M. FRIBA, Letter to The Committee, The Society for the Protection of Ancient Buildings regarding Lydiard Park Mansion, Lydiard Tregoze. (Sept. 1943).

John, David Murray, 'Restoration and Modernisation of Lydiard Park'. A letter to the Chairman and members of the Development Sub-Committee (Sept. 1962).

'My dearest sonne' Letters from the Countess of Rochester to the Earl of Lichfield (University of Rochester).

WSA 2323/15: Correspondence and accounts concerning Ellen Rose St. John natural daughter of Henry Mildmay St. John, 1930-1942.

TNA, PROB 11/47/281: Sir Richard Blount, 1564.

TNA, PROB 11/64/289: Elizabeth Blount, 1582.

TNA, PROB 11/149: Will of the Right Honorable Lady Diana Beauclerk, 1809.

TNA, PROB 11/480: Will of Dame Johanna St. John, 1704

TNA, PROB 11/431: Will of Anne, Countess of Rochester, 1696.

Wiltshire Times, 18 Nov. 1899 p. 6.

Lakes Chronicle, 13 Dec. 1899 p. 7.
Wiltshire Times, 10 March 1922 p. 2.
North Wilts Herald, 28 March 1930 p. 12.
North Wilts Herald, 1 March 1940 p. 12.
North Wilts Herald, 21 March 1941 p. 4.
Swindon Advertiser, 6 Aug. 1943 p.5.
www.histoparl.ac.uk (accessed 2020)
www.oxforddnb.com (accessed 2020)
www.seyntjohn.org.uk (accessed 2020)
www.friendsoflydiardpark.org.uk (accessed 2021)

Guide Books
Lydiard Park and Church. (Swindon Corporation).
Lydiard Park & Church. (Borough of Thamesdown).
Cummings, Sophie, *Lydiard House & Park.* (Swindon Borough Council, 2009).

The Pictures

Portraits (*All courtesy of Lydiard House*)
Lucy Hungerford (p. 36); Barbara St. John (p. 46); Anne Leighton (p. 52 and front cover); Margaret Whitmore (p. 57); Johanna St. John (p. 70); Barbara Villiers (p. 79); Angelica Magdalena Pelissary (p. 89); Frances Winchcomb (p. 94); Marie Claire de Marcilly (p. 100); Henrietta St. John (p. 105); Anne Furnese (p. 113); Diana Spencer (p. 120)

Photographs
Lady Mary E.E. Bolingbroke (p. 135) courtesy of Lydiard House.
Black and white photograph of the back of Lydiard House (p. 130) was provided by the Swindon Society.
All the other photographs are by the author.

Index of Persons and Places

Places are in Wiltshire unless otherwise stated.

Lightning Source UK Ltd.
Milton Keynes UK
UKHW020407080421
381597UK00007B/213